GOD'S WORD
FOR A JR. HIGH WORLD

Christianity: the Basics

Gospel Light

Kara Eckmann Powell

Gospel Light is an evangelical Christian publisher dedicated to serving the local church. We believe God's vision for Gospel Light is to provide church leaders with biblical, user-friendly materials that will help them evangelize, disciple and minister to children, youth and families.

We hope this Gospel Light resource will help you discover biblical truth for your own life and help you minister to youth. God bless you in your work.

For a free catalog of resources from Gospel Light please contact your Christian supplier or contact us at 1-800-4-GOSPEL or at www.gospellight.com.

PUBLISHING STAFF

William T. Greig, Publisher

Dr. Elmer L. Towns, Senior Consulting Publisher

Dr. Gary S. Greig, Senior Consulting Editor

Jill Honodel, Managing Editor

Pam Weston, Editor

Patti Pennington Virtue, Assistant Editor

Christi Goeser, Editorial Assistant

Kyle Duncan, Associate Publisher

Bayard Taylor, M.Div., Senior Editor, Theological and Biblical Issues

Kevin Parks, Cover Designer

Debi Thayer, Designer

Chap Clark, Siv Ricketts and Donna Fitzpatrick, Contributing Writers

How To Make Clean Copies From This Book

You may make copies of portions of this book with a clean conscience if:

- you (or someone in your organization) are the original purchaser;
- you are using the copies you make for a noncommercial purpose (such as teaching or promoting your ministry) within your church or organization;
- you follow the instructions provided in this book.

However, it is ILLEGAL for you to make copies if:

- you are using the material to promote, advertise or sell a product or service other than for ministry fund-raising;
- you are using the material in or on a product for sale;
- you or your organization are **not** the original purchaser of this book.

By following these guidelines you help us keep our products affordable.

Thank you,

Gospel Light

PRAISE FOR PULSE

"**There is a cry from this generation for truth.**" Helen Musick, Youth Specialties National Resource Team member, national speaker and author

"**The Pulse curriculum is truly cross-cultural.**" Walt Mueller, President, Center for Parent/Youth Understanding and author of *Understanding Today's Youth Culture*

"**The creators and writers of this curriculum know and love young teens, and that's what sets [this] curriculum apart from the mediocre stuff!**" Mark Oestreicher, Vice President of Ministry Resources, Youth Specialties

"**Great biblical material, creative interaction and USER FRIENDLY! What more could you ask? I highly recommend it!**" Ken Davis, President, Dynamic Communications International

"**It's about time...curriculum took [junior highers] and...youth workers seriously.**" Rich Van Pelt, Strategic Relationships Director, Compassion International, author, speaker and veteran youth worker

"**A rich resource...that makes genuine connections with middle school students and the culture in which they must live.**" Mark W. Cannister, Ed.D., Chair, Department of Youth Ministries, Gordon College

"**A fresh tool...geared to make a lasting impact.**" Paul Fleischmann, Executive Director, National Network of Youth Ministries

"**This is the best I've seen yet.**" Wayne Rice, author and Junior High Ministry Director, Understanding Your Teenager seminars

"**A landmark resource for years to come.**" Chapman R. Clark, Ph.D., Associate Professor of Youth and Family Ministry, Fuller Theological Seminary

"**It fleshes out...two absolute essentials for great curriculum: biblical depth and active learning.**" Duffy Robbins, Associate Professor, Department of Youth Ministry, Eastern College

"**Pulse...will help God's Word to become real for your students.**" Larry Acosta, President, The Hispanic Ministry Center

"**Pulse will help leaders...bring excellence to every lesson while enjoying the benefit of a simplified preparation time.**" Lynn Ziegenfuss, Vice President of People Development, Youth for Christ/USA

"**Pulse CAPITALIZES both God and Truth.**" Monty L. Hipp, Youth Communicator, Creative Communications

"**The best junior high/middle school curriculum to come out in years.**" Jim Burns, Ph.D., President, Youth Builders

"**Wow! I'm impressed with the quality and message this curriculum brings to the millennials.**" Charles Kim, *JDM—Journey Devotional Magazine*, The Oriental Mission Church

Pulse
Christianity: The Basics

CONTENTSCONTENTSCONTENTSCONTENTSCONTENTS

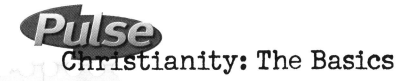

Dedication

To Grandma Eckmann—every visit with you is a lesson in unselfish love and cheerful courage.

And To Grandpa Sutton—hats off for being my model of learning and laughing. When I get older, I want To be like you both.

-Kara

....You've Made the Right Choice in Choosing Pulse for Your Junior Highers

The Top Ten Reasons...

10. Junior highers equate who God is with what church is like. To them a boring youth ministry means a boring God.

Fun and variety are the twin threads that weave their way through this curriculum's every page.

8. Junior highers need ongoing reminders of the big idea of each session.

Wouldn't it be great if you could give your students devotionals every week to reinforce the learning goals of the session? Get this: YOU CAN because THIS CURRICULUM DOES.

9. Junior highers need and deserve youth workers who are expert trainers and teachers of biblical truth.

Every book is pulsating with youth leader tips and a full-length youth worker article designed to infuse YOU with more passion and skill for your ministry to junior highers.

7. Some of our world's most effective evangelists are junior highers.

Every session, and we mean EVERY session, concludes with an evangelism option that ties the "big idea" of the session to the big need to share Christ with others.

6. Since no two junior highers (or their leaders) look, think or act alike, no two junior high ministries look, think or act alike.

   Each step comes with three options that you can cut and paste to create a session that works best for YOUR students and YOUR personality.

5. Junior highers' growing minds are ready for more than just fun and games with a little Scripture thrown in.

   Scripture is the very skeleton of each session, giving it its shape, its form and its very life.

4. Junior highers learn best when they can see, taste, feel and experience the session.

   This curriculum involves students in every step through active learning and games to prove to students that following Christ is the greatest adventure ever.

3. Tragically, most junior highers are under challenged in their walks with Christ.

   We've packed the final step of each session with three options that serve to move students a few steps forward in their walks with Christ.

2. Junior highers tend to understand the Bible in bits and pieces and miss the big picture of all that God has done for them.

   This curriculum follows a strategic three-year plan that walks junior highers through the Bible, stopping at the most important points along the way.

1. Junior highers are moving through all sorts of changes—from getting a new body to getting a new locker.

   We've designed a curriculum that revolves around one simple vision: Moving God's Word into a junior high world.

Moving Through Pulse

Since Pulse is vibrating with so many different learning activities, this guide will help you pick and choose the best possible options for *your* students.

THE SESSIONS

The six sessions are split into two stand-alone units, so you can choose to teach either three or six sessions at a time. Each session is geared to be 45 to 90 minutes long and is comprised of the following four steps.

IT'S YOUR MOVE

A training article for you, the youth worker, to show you *why* and *how* to see students' worlds changed by Christ to change the world.

 **STEP 1** MOVING IN

This first step helps students focus in on the theme of the lesson in a fun and engaging way through three options:

 MOVE IT—An active learning experience that may or may not involve all of your students.

 CHAT ROOM—Provocative, clear and simple questions to get your students thinking and chatting.

 FUN AND GAMES—Zany, creative and competitive games that may or may not involve all of your students.

 **STEP 2** MOVING UP

The second step enables students to look up to God by relating the very words of Scripture to the session topic through three options:

 MOVE IT—An active learning experience that may or may not involve all of your students.

 CHAT ROOM—Provocative, clear and simple questions to get your students chatting about the Scripture lesson.

 PULSE POINTS—A message outline with simple points and meaningful illustrations to give students some massive truths about Scripture with hardly any preparation on your part.

STEP 3 — MOVING ON

This step asks students to look inward and discover how God's Word connects with their own worlds through three options:

 CHAT ROOM—Provocative, clear and simple questions to get your students chatting.

 REAL LIFE—A case study about someone (usually a junior higher) who needs your students' help figuring out what to do.

 TOUGH QUESTIONS—Four to six mind-stretching questions that challenge students to a new level of depth and integration.

STEP 4 — MOVING OUT

This final step leads students out into their world with specific challenges to apply at school, at home and with their friends through three options based on your students' growth potential:

 LIGHT THE FIRE—For junior highers who may or may not be Christians and need easily accessible application ideas.

 FIRED UP—For students who are definitely Christians and are ready for more intense application ideas.

 SPREAD THE FIRE—A special evangelism application idea for students with a passion to see others come to know Christ.

OTHER IMPORTANT MOVING PARTS

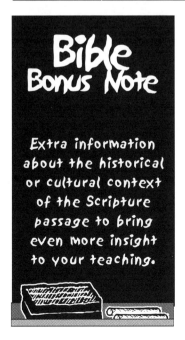

Bible Bonus Note

Extra information about the historical or cultural context of the Scripture passage to bring even more insight to your teaching.

Youth Leader Tip

Suggestions, options and/or other useful information to make your life easier—or at least more interesting!

Devotions in Motion

WEEK FIVE: GRACE

Four devotionals for each session so that the big idea keeps moving through your junior highers' lives all week long.

ON THE MOVE—An appealing, easy-to-read handout you can give your junior highers to make sure they learn all the basics of Christianity.

Junior Highers and the Bible: Why Bother?

BY CHAP CLARK

Brad got in trouble with your church's security guard, again.

Davison punched a hole in your youth-room wall.

Teresa ditched her small group.

In the midst of this Wednesday night chaos, you tried to teach about the difference between creation and evolution. Now you're driving home, battling with the same old weekly question: What difference did that last 90 minutes with these junior highers make in anyone's life?

But here's the great paradox of junior high ministry: We find out later that they heard, observed and processed much more information than we ever thought possible! We who actually work with this age group are well aware that there is much more to each of these young souls and minds than what we see on Sunday mornings and Wednesday nights.

They are emerging as thinkers. They are constantly changing and being challenged by life, friends, love and parents; and they want to know what God has to say about all of this. Thus, even though we may be feeling like our lessons are bombing, an emerging axiom of junior high ministry is that we must teach these early adolescents how to reflect theologically as followers of Jesus Christ.

They are capable, if only in short little blips, of interacting with Scripture, of wrestling with God and of deep intimate relationships with the One who loves them best. Allow me to suggest three goals for every time you teach junior highers.

It's Your Move

TO BUILD YOUNG THEOLOGIANS

Theological reflection sounds far more ominous than it really is. Theological reflection simply means that we teach our students that God cares about them, their lives and their world *and* that He passionately wants to communicate to them through His Word and the Holy Spirit. There are no areas of their lives that can (or should) be fenced off from their relationships with Christ.

TO BRING THE BIBLE TO LIFE

The Bible, then, is not just about stories and rules, but rather it is a comprehensive love letter in which God speaks to the souls of—even—junior highers. When we teach students how to meditate on the Word of God and how to look for the living God in its pages, they will be able to see the Christian faith as something that actually will make a difference in their day-to-day lives.

TO HELP THEM SHARE THEIR FAITH

The number-one task of youth ministry—or ministry to any age group—is to draw students into a personal, trusting faith in Jesus Christ. Our task is not about classes or programs or games; it is about seeing God connect with students in a way that changes them forever. But that is not our task alone, it's our students' too. As your students have that "Aha!" experience of understanding the basics of Christianity, they'll want to invite their friends to experience the incredible ride of following Christ, too. The things we do—the fun, the interaction, the teaching—are simply tools to bring students like Brad, Davison and Teresa to a place of warm interest and wild devotion to the God who has come for them. Good theology does that!

Contributors

Dr. Chap Clark, Ph.D. is The Associate Professor of Youth and Family Ministries at Fuller Theological Seminary, a member of The Youth Specialties Resource Seminar Team and executive pastor at Glendale Presbyterian Church in Glendale, California.

Siv Ricketts, author of The Bible Bonus Notes is a Student Ministries Director, freelance writer and editor living in San Diego, California. Siv and her husband, Dave, have been ministering To students Together for The past six years and have recently been blessed with a new son, Corban.

Donna Fitzpatrick, author of The student article, "How Can I Get To Know Jesus?" lives in Northern California with her husband, Dan, and seven of her eight children. With The oldest in her Third year of college and The youngest in her Third year of age, life is never dull! Donna enjoys writing, public speaking and home schooling.

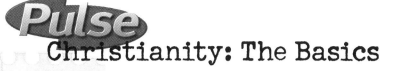

SESSIONONESESSIONONESESSIONONESESSIONONE

The Big Idea

God is our heavenly Father who loves us no matter what we do.

Session Aims

In this session you will guide students to:

- Learn what Luke 15 teaches about the Father's "no matter what" love;
- Experience relief and joy that, unlike everyone else, their heavenly Father loves them at all times and in all places;
- Respond by identifying one way that remembering their Father's love will help them feel OK this week.

The Biggest Verse

"But while he was still a long way off, his father saw him and was filled with compassion for him; he ran to his son, threw his arms around him and kissed him." Luke 15:20

Other Important Verses

Luke 12:6,7; 15:11-32; John 13:34,35; 17:23; Romans 8:38,39

God the Father: The Love

STEP
MOVING IN

This step reminds us that love is something we all want—and boy, do we want it badly!

Option 1 — Move It

You'll need A copy of this week's "Top 20" list of songs from your community's most popular contemporary radio station.

Greet students and introduce this new series to them. Then explain that they're going to have a "Super Sing Off."

Divide students into two teams based on what kind of shoes they're wearing. **Note:** Since we don't know what kind of shoes your students will be wearing, you're going to have to make this call—maybe by whether or not they have shoelaces, or tennis shoes versus everyone else, or something even more relevant to your own students.

Explain that you will yell a word or phrase and then point to one of the two teams. Someone from that team must run to the front of the room and lead his or her team in 10 seconds of a song that has that word or phrase in it. Secular songs, worship songs and commercial jingles are all fair game. After the song is sung, that person sits down. Then you point to the second team and they likewise have one person run forward and lead in a song with the word you have yelled out. This goes back and forth until one team gets stumped, at which point you award points to the other team and yell out the next word.

The words, in their recommended order, are as follows:

  rock
  car (or a type of car)
  any number
  arm or hand
  any color
  love

When you're finished with all six words, congratulate the winning team. Read the songs titles from the Top 20 list and ask: **What are the most popular themes in these song titles?** Hopefully, love will be one of the first things mentioned, but if not, introduce it yourself and ask: **Why**

are love and relationships such common themes? What does this say about what people want? Where do people tend to look to find love? How long does that kind of love last?

Transition to the next step by explaining: **Today we're going to study the most perfect type of love that could possibly exist. It's the only type of love that can meet our ultimate need for love and that will last forever.**

Option 2 — Chat Room

You'll need Zippo, nothing, just yourself and this book!

Greet students and explain that this new series is all about the basics of being a Christian, then ask: **What are some of the most basic things you need in order to live?** Students' answers will certainly include food, water and a place to live. Explain that the following true story points to one of our most basic needs that we don't always realize we have.

In a high school classroom, 11 students sat in chairs arranged in a circle, playing a game called Lifeboat. The leader said, "Imagine that you're the only survivors of a shipwreck and you have crawled into a lifeboat that can only hold 10 people. Now you've got to decide who should jump overboard and drown so that the rest of you can live."

And so they began to go around the circle, talking about each person. Juan was a straight-*A* student and they decided his death would be a tremendous waste of intellect. Clara, the cheerleader, was selected to remain immediately. No reasons were given, but everyone knew that a girl with her looks couldn't be eliminated. Sam, the starting quarterback, was kept because of his great contributions on the field. And then the spotlight fell on Anne.

Slightly overweight, not blessed with many nice clothes, she had always been just one of the faces in the crowd. There was a moment of silence, each person waiting for someone else to come up with a reason why Anne shouldn't be sacrificed. No one could think of anything and finally one student blurted out, "And Anne, well, she shouldn't jump either."

The game continued and the students couldn't decide who should jump overboard. At a standstill, Anne finally ended the game with, "I'll jump."

The group thanked her for her sacrifice, but

Anne wasn't listening. She was thinking about another message she heard from them. Several days later when it wasn't just a game, she did jump—to her death.

Continue: **This is a heartbreaking story, but it helps us think about how tough it is when we don't feel loved and supported. In fact, research and interviews indicate that the one thing people want more than anything else is to be loved.** Do you agree with this? What do people tend to do in order to feel loved? How long does this work?

Today we're going to study the most important and best kind of love ever, and it's not based on how our friends feel about us.

Option 3  Fun and Games

You'll need A TV, a VCR, a blank videotape and a copy of *TV Guide.*

Ahead of time, record three minutes of the corniest infomercial you can find. (If you don't have cable, tape three consecutive minutes of commercials as a **low-tech** option.) Watch the video clip and come up with 10 trivia questions, such as, "What color watch was the woman wearing?" or "What did they offer after the promise: 'But wait, there's more'?"

Welcome students and explain that you're launching a new series today, and to kick it off you need three volunteers who like to watch television.

Gather the volunteers in the front of the room and explain that you're going to play three minutes of an infomercial (or commercials) for them. They need to pay attention because afterward you are going to be asking them trivia questions. If any of the three contestants knows the answer to the question, he should raise his hand; then give his answer once you call on him. If he raises his hand before you finish reading the question, immediately stop reading and have him give his answer. If his answer is wrong, continue to read the question and ask one of the other volunteers to respond. If none of the contestants has the right answer, ask the audience. After all 10 questions have been answered, give the winning contestant a copy of *TV Guide* as a prize.

Discuss:

What are some of your favorite infomercials or commercials?

What is the purpose of commercials? The ultimate focus of commercials is that they are trying to help people feel loved. That's why they try to sell things such as acne cream that will make your skin glow or a gym membership that will cause the girls to flock to your buff 13-year-old body.

Explain: **Today we're going to study something that isn't advertised on television but meets our need to feel loved. You can't order it from television, but you can walk away with it today for free.**

This step teaches that God's love for us is a "no matter what" love.

Option 1  Move It

You'll need Your Bible.

Ask for seven volunteers, then assign the volunteers the following roles: father, older son, younger son, two pigs and two servants. If you have fewer than seven students, ask some to play multiple roles, which could make this even more humorous.

Explain: **The Bible is very alive and exciting and today we're going to act out a fun story that comes word for word from the Bible.** Explain that these seven volunteers are to do exactly what the story says and the rest of the students are the audience whose main job is to cheer on the student actors.

Make sure that the student you assign as the "younger son" is fairly dramatic and self-confident. You play the part of the narrator and read Luke 15:11-32 one verse at a time in a very animated voice, letting students act out the story one verse at a time. Also, if any character has a speaking part that is more than six words, have her move her lips as if she were repeating the lines—we call this "Godzilla-movie style." When you are finished, give the actors some major applause.

Continue: **Parables are stories with meaning; and the key to understanding any parable is to understand the actions, motives and symbolism of the main characters.** Discuss the following:

In Jesus' parable, who does the father stand for? God.

Who do the sons stand for? Us.

Why did the younger son return?

Why did the older son resent the father's love?

What is the difference between the two sons? The younger one was surprised that the father loved him *no matter what*, and he didn't even have to deliver the speech he had rehearsed (see vv. 18,19). The older son resented his father's love toward his younger brother because he felt his brother didn't deserve it because the younger brother had blown it.

When might kids you know feel resentment toward someone who loves another person unconditionally? If students seem open to discussing times when they themselves have felt like the younger (or older) son, press in and ask them.

Option 2
Chat Room

You'll need Several Bibles.

Ask students if they've ever wondered about the answers to the following *why* questions:

Why are there interstate highways in Hawaii?

If nothing ever sticks to Teflon, why does Teflon stick to the pan?

Why do they put braille dots on the keypad of drive-up ATMs?

Why do we drive on parkways and park on driveways?

Why is it that when adults are driving and looking for an address, they turn down the volume on the radio?

You know that little indestructible black box that is used on the planes—why can't they make the whole plane out of the same substance?

If 7-11 is open 24 hours a day, 365 days a year, why are there locks on the door?

Distribute Bibles and explain that one of the most important questions we can ask about any story in the Bible is *why* the people in the story do what they do. Read Luke 15:11-32, then ask:

Why did the younger son leave and then return to his dad? Because he was independent and wanted to try living on his own.

Why did the dad welcome him back? Because he loved him.

Why did the older son resent his younger brother? Because he had chosen to stick around to work and remain loyal to his dad, but his brother got the hero's welcome after messing up his life and losing his inheritance.

Why did the sons respond differently? The younger son appreciated God's love once he came back home; the older son took his dad's love for granted. Explain that the key to understanding parables is understanding who the characters represent.

Who does the younger son represent in the story? He represents us.

Who is the dad in the story? The dad represents God.

Why is this story important to us? Share that it is God's amazing love that motivates Him to welcome us back into relationship with Him, even after we've done some stupid or wrong things. No matter what we've done, He's waiting to have a relationship with us.

Bible Bonus Note

The Nature of the Parable:

The word "parable" comes from the Greek word *parabole*, meaning "putting things side by side." Jesus did not intend the parables to be understood literally, but used them to jolt His audience into seeing things differently, forcing them to decide about Him and His message and to act accordingly. Jesus took illustrations for the parables from nature, familiar customs or events, and everyday life—things that His audience could easily understand and apply.

Option 3  Pulse Points

You'll need Several Bibles, a chopstick or small piece of wood or twig, a two-by-four piece of lumber approximately three feet in length or a similarly unbreakable piece of wood.

The Big Idea

God loves us with a no-matter-what love.

The Big Question

What is this no-matter-what love like?

1. God's love is unimaginable.

Ask students if they would still be friends with someone if that someone:

- **Ditched your birthday party.**
- **Spread a rumor that you had cheated on a history test.**
- **Wouldn't stop calling you a really embarrassing nickname.**
- **Borrowed your favorite jacket, then claimed that they hadn't.**
- **Hung out with the popular kids at school most of the time and only paid attention to you when the popular students were not around.**

Most of us would probably break friendships at any one of these points, but God's love is different. We can't even imagine how huge His love is, but we can get an idea from Luke 15.

2. God's love is unbreakable.

Place the chopstick and the two-by-four nearby. Read Luke 15:11-32 and explain: **Even though the younger son wanted his inheritance, implying that he didn't care whether his dad was alive or dead, the dad welcomed him back. Our love for others is often like a chopstick.** Hold up the chopstick, and as you snap it in half, share that our love for others can be easily broken. Hold up the two-by-four and compare it with God's love for us which can't be broken like the chopstick can.

Continue: **Not only did the son disrespect his dad, but he hung out with pigs, which in his family's Jewish culture was one of the worst insults ever. Yet the dad didn't turn his back on his son. He welcomed him home with open arms and gifts. That is how God loves us—unconditionally.**

Youth Leader Tip

In every discussion, go for the real stuff. That means talking about real issues and real struggles instead of just looking for the Sunday School answers. You can often go deeper if you move from the general to the personal by first asking students to comment on what their friends might think/experience/feel before asking them about their own lives. Generally, junior highers will match your level of authenticity but will not exceed it. You set the tone by being real.

STEP 3
MOVING ON

This step helps us feel secure knowing that God loves us equally at all times and in all places.

Option 1 Chat Room

You'll need A video camera, a blank videotape, a TV and a VCR.

Ahead of time, carry a video camera with you for an entire day. Videotape yourself (using either a tripod or someone who is with you) in all sorts of settings during a typical day: waking up, brushing your teeth, eating breakfast, driving, working at the office, eating lunch, talking on the phone, working out and watching TV. Try to make the video as humorous, unpredictable and zany as possible. Make sure to tape yourself reading Scripture or walking into church, for these will be important points in your discussion.

A low-tech alternative: Simply ask students what they do during an average day, making sure to add some ideas from a typical Sunday.

Introduce this step by explaining that you want to give students an up-close-and-personal look at a typical day in your life. Play the video, then discuss the following:

When in my day does God love me the most? Does God love me more when I'm praying than eating? The truth is that God loves us equally at all times and in all places. Read Romans 8:38,39 as proof of His love.

Would God love a criminal who murdered a family on their way home from church as much as He loves me? Yes. Although God would be angry at the sin, He still loves all people and all sinners equally.

If my neighbor tells me that she hates God, does God still love her? Yes. Although God may feel sad, this isn't going to stop His love.

If God loves us no matter what, can we do anything we want? God loves us just as we are, but He loves us so much He wants us to change and be transformed into His image. Ask: **In one word, explain how God's no-matter-what love makes you feel.**

Option 2 Real Life

You'll need Five copies of "Love-O-Meter" (pp. 23-24).

Ahead of time, give copies of the "Love-O-Meter" script to five students so they can practice their parts in advance.

Introduce this step by explaining that this drama is one way people view God and His love. When the drama is finished, thank the student actors and ask: **Given what we learned from Luke 15, what do you think of the message of this drama?** Read Romans 8:38,39 and continue: **Considering Luke 15 and Romans 8:38,39, what would you say to Marco if you were his friend Andy?**

Option 3 Tough Questions

You'll need A willingness to wrestle with students about the truth about God.

1. **Does God love Christians and non-Christians equally?** Yes, He loves all people with the same amount of love.
2. **Does God love Christians who obey Him more than Christians who disobey Him?** No, the ground is level at the cross of Jesus Christ. **Why?** Because we are all sinners before our holy God and He loved us so much He gave His Son to die for us. He loves us all equally.
3. **If God loves all people equally, why are some people poor and others rich, and why do some people go through tough stuff when other people have everything work out great?** These situations do not reflect discrepancies in God's love. He loves us enough to allow unique circumstances to teach us each important lessons about what it means to follow and obey Him.
4. **Is it possible for us to love another person with the same no-matter-what love that God has for us?** Well, never as perfectly as God does, but imitating Him is always our goal.

STEP 4

MOVING OUT

This step points out ways our Father's love can be felt even though being a junior higher is really hard.

Option 1  Light the Fire

You'll need One dime per student.

Introduce this step by explaining that although our heavenly Father's love for us is bigger and better than we can imagine, we can get glimpses of it. Then read the following humorous story:

> Joe, a college student, was taking a class to learn about birds. The night before the final exam, Joe spent all night studying. He had the textbook practically memorized. He knew his class notes backward and forward. Joe was ready.
>
> The morning of the test, Joe entered the auditorium and took a seat in the front row. On the table in the front was a row of 10 stuffed birds. Each bird had a sack covering its body, and only its legs were showing. When class started, the professor announced that the students were to identify each bird by looking at its legs and giving its common name, habitat, preferred food, mating habits, etc.
>
> Joe looked at each of the birds' legs. They all looked the same to him. He started to get angry. He had stayed up all night studying for this test and now he had to identify birds by their legs. The more he thought about the situation, the angrier he got. Finally he reached his boiling point. He stood up, marched up to the professor's desk, crumpled up his exam paper and threw it on the desk. "What a ridiculous test!" he told the prof. "How could anyone tell the difference between these birds by looking at their legs?"
>
> With that, Joe turned and stormed toward the exit. The professor was a bit shocked, and it took him a moment to regain his composure. Then, just as Joe was about to walk out the door, the prof shouted out, "Wait a minute, young man, what's your name?"
>
> Joe turned around, pulled up his pant legs and hollered, "You tell me, prof, you tell me!"[1]

Ask for a volunteer to read Luke 12:6,7. Comment on how amazing it is that our loving heavenly Father knows everything about us, including the number of hairs on our head and what our legs look like. Share: **God not only knows what we look like, but He likes what we look like. It's often tough to feel His love if we don't like how He's made us, especially if we don't like how we look.**

As students are leaving your room, distribute a dime to each student as a reminder of the truth that they're a perfect 10. (Aren't you relieved we recommend a dime and not a $10 bill per student?)

Youth Leader Tip

Even if you are telling a humorous story, it's best not to introduce it as such. When you start by saying, "This is such a funny story; you guys are going to love it," you've instantly raised students' expectations higher than your story may be able to reach. It's safer and better to simply say you have a story to share. Then whether students just smile or roar with laughter at the end, it is equally OK.

Option 2 — Fired Up

You'll need Paper and pens or pencils.

Divide students into groups of five or six. Distribute a paper and a pencil to each group and ask one student from each group who most recently celebrated his or her birthday to be that group's note taker.

Ask the group to brainstorm the top five toughest things about being a junior higher. Once they have agreed on the top five things, have the note taker in each group write the list down on paper.

Each group should then hand its paper to another group so they now have another group's list of the "Top Five Toughest Things About Being a Junior Higher." Next to each tough thing, the group should write one way that knowing our heavenly Father's love can make us feel OK in the midst of that tough situation.

Following the principle of moving from the general to the personal (see Youth Leader Tip, p. 19), ask students to share within their small groups one tough thing they will face this week. Then each group member should give a one-sentence explanation of how knowing our heavenly Father's love will help that student feel OK in the midst of what they're going through. (It's perfectly OK if some group members duplicate what others have already said.)

Close the session by asking the small groups to pray together that each of them will remember how much God loves them during their tough times in the coming week.

Option 3 — Spread the Fire

You'll need A shoebox covered with wrapping paper or aluminum foil, pens or pencils and copies of "Encouragement" (p. 25). Cut the encouragement "cards" apart.

Explain: **We can play a part in helping others to know about our heavenly Father's love.** Ask two volunteers to read John 13:34,35 and two volunteers to read John 17:23. Ask: **What difference does the way we share God's love with each other make in helping others come to know God's love?** Be sure to explain that in the context of these passages, Jesus is talking about the way Christians love each other, not the way Christians love non-Christians.

Create a picture in the students' minds of what it means to love each other in your junior high ministry by explaining that gossip would end, judging would end and sarcasm would end. In place of the negatives, encouragement, acceptance and friendship would explode. Ask: **How is this different from what your friends at school are used to?**

Continue: **Today we are going to take a major step toward that through a new "Encouragement Box."** Hand out copies of "Encouragement" and pens or pencils to students. Ask them to write two or three notes to others in your ministry who need a little bit of encouragement today. After you have given them five minutes to do this, collect the papers, shuffle them in the box and distribute them.

Note:
1. Adapted from Jim Burns and Greg McKinnon, *Fresh Ideas: Illustrations, Stories and Quotes* (Ventura CA: Gospel Light, 1997), pp. 31-32.

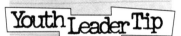

Youth Leader Tip

Be sure to have adult staff members write letters to students who might not be as likely to receive a letter from anyone else so that this exercise doesn't create any "I-feel-like-a-loner-and-nobody-likes-me" feelings. Consider keeping the box out during future meetings so students can write letters to each other before and after the meetings.

Love-O-Meter

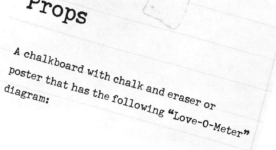

Props

A chalkboard with chalk and eraser or poster that has the following "Love-O-Meter" diagram:

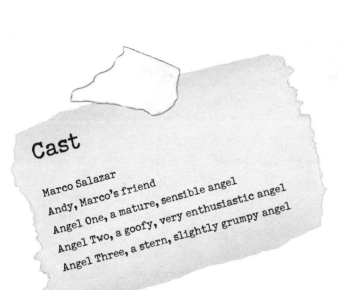

Cast

Marco Salazar

Andy, Marco's friend

Angel One, a mature, sensible angel

Angel Two, a goofy, very enthusiastic angel

Angel Three, a stern, slightly grumpy angel

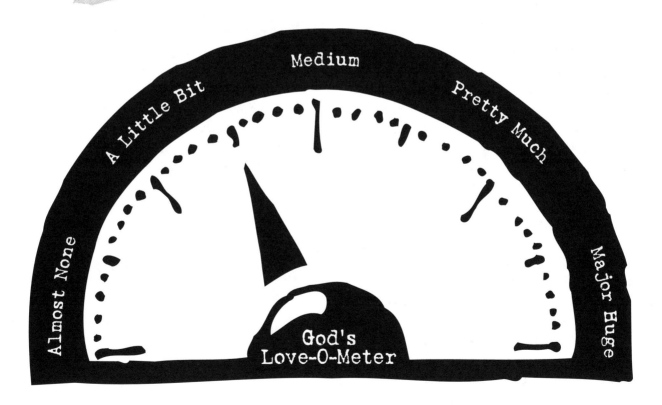

Love-O-Meter

Marco: Hey Andy, how's it going?

Andy: OK, although I've got a ton of homework.

Marco: Me too, and since I go to this new Christian school, I have to write about the Bible and God and stuff. Today my homework assignment is to write a one-page essay about God's love for me. It's going to take me forever because I'm sort of confused about God's love. Like here's what I think… (*Marco and Andy pause as the three angels enter and begin their discussion in another part of the room near the Love-O-Meter diagram.*)

Angel Two: (*Turns to Angel One and extends hand.*) Greetings! I'm the angel in charge of the "good-stuff-teens-do" department, reporting for work. (*Turns slightly to the audience, winks and whispers.*) It's my first day on the job.

Angel Three: (*Shaking hand of Angel One firmly.*) Hello, I'm the angel in charge of the "not-so-good-stuff-teens-do" department, reporting for work. I'm a veteran of this job.

Angel One: It's heavenly to be working with both of you. I'm the angel in charge of God's Love-O-Meter. (*Points to Love-O-Meter.*) We have the following categories to show how much God loves us: Almost None, A Little Bit, Medium, Pretty Much and Major Huge. Right now we're going to discuss Marco Salazar's afternoon reading. Let's do a quick review. Both of you need to give me a rundown on Marco's behavior. I will adjust the dial on the Love-O-Meter accordingly. Where we finish at the end will be the amount of love he is receiving today. As you probably remember at the end of our noon meter scoring, Marco ended with "A Little Bit" of love based on his talking in class when he was supposed to be listening to his teacher.

Angel Two: I'd like to point out that at lunchtime at Marco's school, a girl dropped her tray of food and he helped her pick up the stuff even though he thought his friends would probably make fun of him. That would put him up to "Major Huge" love, right?

Angel One: (*Gently sarcastic.*) I don't think so. Marco's score will reach "Pretty Much" love, but no higher.

Angel Three: However, as soon as he got home, he started bugging his little brother and caused him to start screaming…

Angel One: Tut, tut, tut. (*Moves the dial to "A Little Bit."*)

Angel Three: While his mom was trying to talk on the phone.

Angel One: Oh… (*Moves the dial to "Almost None."*)

Angel Two: But, after he got in trouble for that, he put away the dishes without being asked, which I think should bring him up to "Pretty Much" love.

Angel One: (*Sarcastic.*) Yeah, right. The fact is that will take him to "Medium" love.

Angel Three: However, when his mother read the note from the teacher about the talking in class problem and she sat Marco down to talk about it, he talked back to her.

Angel One: Whoops. (*Moves the dial to "A Little Bit."*)

Angel Two: But when he was sent to his room, he started on his homework without being told. That has to bring him back up to "Pretty Much" love.

Angel One: That's absolutely right—NOT! It is very obvious that this is your first day on the job. Actually, it will take him to "Medium" love and that is where he stops for this afternoon. (*Angels freeze and Marco and Andy resume action.*)

Andy: Wow, that's pretty intense.

Marco: Well, that's what I think. Do you think I'm right?

Marco, Andy and the angels exit the stage.[2]

Note:
2. Adapted from Jim Burns, Christine Stanfield and Joe Lusz, *Fresh Ideas: Skits & Dramas* (Ventura CA: Gospel Light, 1998), pp. 30-33.

Encouragement

"By This all...will Know ThaT you are my disciples, if you love one anoTher." John 13:35

Encouragement

"By This all...will Know ThaT you are my disciples, if you love one anoTher." John 13:35

Encouragement

"By This all...will Know ThaT you are my disciples, if you love one anoTher." John 13:35

Devotions in Motion

DAY 1

FAST FACTS

If There's something about how you look that you don't really like, you'll love these fast facts from Genesis 1:1 —2:3.

God Says

Well, first there's the bump on your nose. And then there's your frizzy hair. And of course, you can't forget the two mountainous moles on your cheek. Every time you look in your mirror, that's all you see: bumps, frizz and moles.

God is your creator. He made you, bumps, frizz and all. He spent a ton of time making sure the earth, animals, plants and water were right in the beginning, and he spent a lot of time making sure you were just right. Nothing about you is a mistake. You are his perfect creation. He looks at you and says, "Wow, that's good. Better than good, that's really good. Better than really good, that's perfect!"

I Do

Maybe it's not bumps, frizz and moles, but you probably have a few things you'd like to change about yourself if you could. Today when you look in the mirror, remember that God thinks it's all good. Since the God who created you thinks you look good, maybe you should too.

FOLD HERE

DAY 4

FAST FACTS

Finding out more about God is easy if you read 1 John 4:7-18.

God Says

Fill in the blank: Verse 16 sets up the following equation:

God equals _____

What is the best description of God's love?

☐ Windy: It goes where it wants to, but you can never count on it.

☐ Sunny: It's with you only when life is good and easy.

☐ Stormy: It's quick to get revenge on you when you do something wrong.

☐ None of the above.

How would you define God's love?

Since God is perfect love, what should happen to our fear?

I Do

What is your biggest fear? The next time you start to feel afraid, remember that thinking about God makes all fear totally disappear.

What is something you could do today for someone in your family to let them know how much you love them?

QUICK QUESTIONS

To read one of the craziest stories in the Bible, turn to Hosea 3:1.

God Says

Just to give you a bit of background: Hosea is this really cool guy who knew God wanted him to marry Gomer. Gomer, in addition to having a pretty strange name for a woman, kept leaving Hosea to go sleep with other men (sounds like a scriptural soap opera, doesn't it?) What commands does God give Hosea in Hosea 3:1?

- ☐ Go, show and love.
- ☐ Stop, drop and roll.
- ☐ Shake, rattle and roll.

What does this tell you about how the Israelites were acting?

How does God respond to the Israelites, even though they're hanging out with other "loser" gods?

I Do

What does Hosea 3:1 say about how much God loves you, even when you may be doing some pretty lame stuff?

FOLD HERE

FAST FACTS

Read Romans 8:38,39 quickly, then check out these fast facts.

God Says

You wish you had never heard of Kansas City. Actually, you hadn't until your best friend told you that her dad had gotten a new construction job in Kansas City and the whole family was moving. Now she's hundreds of miles away in a whole other state and you're left alone. You really miss all that you and your best bud used to do together, especially biking home from school and talking in computer chat rooms.

God's never going to move away from you to Kansas City—or any place else for that matter. He's never going to remove his love from you. It's permanent and goes with you wherever you go.

I Do

Think of everything you're going to do today: First, you'll get ready for school...then have breakfast...then bike to school. Take tests...eat in the cafeteria...go to piano practice...talk on the phone...have dinner...watch television...and finally, go to bed. God's with you through every part of that. Think of the part of the day that is your least favorite and picture God sitting right next to you as you're taking your English test or running laps at soccer practice. Any time you feel sad or lonely this week, think of God sitting right next to you whispering how much He loves you.

The Big Idea

Jesus Christ is the one true way to have a friendship with God.

Session Aims

In this lesson you will guide students to:

- Understand that in the midst of this age of relativism, Jesus is not a liar, nor a lunatic, but the Lord;
- Experience the freedom that comes from asking God to forgive their sins;
- Respond by asking Christ to be their Savior and Lord.

The Biggest Verse

"Jesus answered, 'I am the way and the truth and the life. No one comes to the Father except through me.'" John 14:6

Other Important Verses

John 6:35; 8:12; 10:11,14,15; 15:5; 18:28-40; Romans 3:23; 6:23; 1 Peter 3:15,16

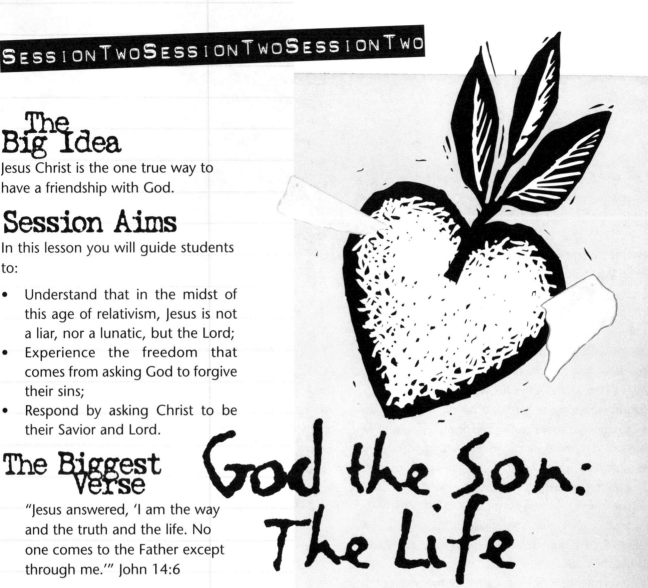

God the Son: The Life

STEP
MOVING IN

This step shows students the importance of knowing the truth.

Option 1 Move It

You'll need One M&M candy per student with equal numbers of red, blue, yellow, green, orange and brown M&Ms, a 3x5-inch index card and pens or pencils.

Welcome students and give each one an M&M. Have each put the M&M in his or her mouth and leave it open so that the color can be seen. (That ought to cut down on a lot of talking for a few minutes!) Have students find everyone else in the room who has the same color as they do, then sit down. If students are in groups of more than 10, have them divide into subgroups within the color. If they are in groups of less than 5, have them combine groups.

Distribute an index card and pencil to each student. Have them write down one lie and one truth about themselves on their index cards without letting anybody else see what they have written. You may need to give an example from your own life, such as you lived in Kenya, you hate dogs or you can burp the alphabet (a show-stopping trick in any junior high ministry!).

Have each group collect its own cards, shuffle them and put them face down in the center of the circle. Have the group members pick one card from the center of their circle and try to guess whose card it is. Once they've guessed the correct person, have them try to guess which statement is the truth and which is the lie. Once everybody in the circle has guessed, have the person whose card it is share the correct answer. Continue this process with each group member. Ask each group to keep track of who guesses the truths and lies most accurately.

Ask the winner from each group: **How did you know what was the truth?** If the answer is that it was a lucky guess, reinforce the importance of using our minds to try to figure out the truth. If the answer is that it was because they knew the other students in their group, emphasize how much easier it is to figure out the truth about someone if we already know them.

Ask students: **When is it easier to know the truth: when we're children, junior highers or adults? Now that you're in junior high, why is it important to know the truth about stuff?** Take a moment to explain that today's culture is hip-deep in relativism—the belief that truth doesn't really exist and isn't really important at all. This means that whatever people want to believe is true can be true for them, which isn't really truth at all.

Discuss: **How can we get better at figuring out what the truth is?**

What is the most important truth in the whole world?

Explain: **Truth doesn't change, isn't voted upon and is the same for everyone. Today we're going to study the best and most important truth of all—the true Way to God.**

Option 2 Chat Room

You'll need Zippo, nada, absolutely nothing.

Greet students warmly and explain that today you have some tricky questions and that they will all need to work together to figure out the true answers. One at a time, read the questions from the following list, and ask students for their guesses about the true answer before you read the actual answer.

1. **Do they have a Fourth of July in England?** Yes, and they also have a first, second and third of July, etc.
2. **Some months have 31 days; how many have 28?** All months have at least 28 days.
3. **Why can't a man living in the United States be buried in Canada?** Because he is still living.
4. **How many outs are there in an inning?** Six, three per side.
5. **If there are three apples and you take two, how many do you have?** Two—you just took two apples.
6. **If you have only one match and you walk into a room where there is an oil burner, a kerosene lamp and a wood burning stove, which one would you light first?** You'd have to light the match first.
7. **A farmer has 17 sheep and all but 9 die. How many are left?** Nine—all but nine died.
8. **How many animals of each sex did Moses take on the ark?** None—Moses was not on the ark.
9. **How many two-cent stamps are there in a dozen?** 12.
10. **How much dirt is in a hole three feet wide by five**

feet long by four feet deep? None, there's no dirt in a hole.

After you have finished this "truth" quiz, discuss:

Why was it hard to know the true answers?

Who might do better at figuring out the true answers to this type of question: second graders or junior highers?

Why are junior highers better at figuring out the truth?

If you could find out the true answer to any question, what question would you like to ask?

After a few answers are shared, explain: **Today we're going to find out the true answer to the question, How do we get to God?—the most important question in the whole world.**

Option 3  Fun and Games

You'll need Several large trash bags, tape, a plastic tarp, a hose and a bucket of water.

> **CAUTION**
> To prevent this from being a very quick *and* rather traumatic game, poke a hole ahead of time in each of the bags used to cover students' heads.

Ahead of time, think of two good male friends and two good female friends in your youth ministry. Pick one of the males and one of the females and interview them ahead of time by asking them the following questions and writing down their answers:

> What is your favorite TV show?
> What is your nickname?
> If you could eat dinner at one restaurant every Friday, which would it be?
> What is your middle name?
> What is the music group you listen to the most?
> What is your favorite thing to do after school?
> What is your favorite computer game or web site?
> What cartoon character do you hate the most?

Rewrite the answers to their questions into sentences, such as "Jed's favorite TV show is the Weather Channel highlights" or "Mabel's middle name is Gertrude." Make approximately half of the sentences based on true answers and the other half based on lies.

Greet students and thank them for being with you today. Congratulate them on the ways they are trying to build friendships with each other and say that there are two friendships you've noticed recently. Call out the names of the two boys and two girls you've thought of ahead of time. Take the boy and girl you did *not* interview and have them cover themselves with trash bags, placing one trash bag over each of their heads and one for each of their legs. Tape the bags together around their waists to create a waterproof costume.

Ask your "well bagged" female to stand on the tarp as you read through the statements one at a time, asking her to figure out whether it is a truth or a lie. For every answer she gets right, congratulate her for knowing the truth. For every answer she gets wrong, explain that she missed the truth and dump a bucket of water on her. Repeat this process with the well-bagged male student.

> **LESS MESSY OPTION:** If this is a little over-the-top-messy for your setting, squirt her with a squirt gun instead.

Explain that although today the results of not knowing the truth were obvious, they're not always easy to see so quickly. Ask students to share some potentially painful consequences of not knowing the truth. Answers may include: you do something stupid, you get hurt or you hurt other people.

Take a moment to explain: **Today's culture is hip-deep in relativism—the belief that truth doesn't really exist and all truth is relative. This means that whatever people want to believe is true can be true for them, that what's true for one isn't necessarily true for all and that truth changes depending on the situation—none of which is really truth at all! Today we're going to study the most important truth of all—the true Way to God.**

NOTES

STEP 2 — MOVING UP

The goal of this step is to show students that Jesus is not a liar, nor a lunatic, but the true Lord.

Option 1 — Move It

You'll need Several Bibles, three copies of "Liar, Lunatic or Lord Debate" (p. 38), a video camera, a blank videotape, a TV and a VCR. (**Low tech version:** Substitute a cassette recorder and a blank cassette tape for the video equipment .)

Ahead of time, head to a local shopping mall and record teenagers' responses to the following two questions: What is truth? What does Jesus have to do with the truth? You'll invariably get some strange responses and that's the point of this discussion, as you will soon see.

Also ahead of time, give a copy of "Liar, Lunatic or Lord Debate" to three adults. Each of them should choose one position—liar, lunatic or Lord—so that they can prepare arguments ahead of time based on some of the ideas listed on the handout.

Show the video recording to students (or play the cassette) and discuss:

What are some of the answers on the tape that you think are wrong?

What are some of the answers on the tape that you think are true?

Explain: **People have been trying to figure out what the truth is for a long time.** Distribute Bibles and ask students to turn to John 18:28-40. Ask for a volunteer to read the part of the narrator, another to read the words of Pilate and a third to read the words of Christ. Everyone else is part of the crowd.

Continue: **Both the people in the shopping mall and Pilate were trying to figure out the truth. Today we're going to have a great debate to try to figure out what is true.** You will serve as the moderator and read some of Jesus' most controversial statements—statements that were bound to perplex people like Pilate. In addition, you will ask three adults to share some ideas on what those statements mean. Introduce the three adults and ask them to state which position they have chosen: liar, lunatic or Lord.

One at a time, read the verses from John and let the three adults debate whether they prove Jesus was a liar, a lunatic or Lord. After you have finished, ask students to take a vote to decide which arguments make the most sense. Call on some students to share the reason(s) for their positions.

Reread John 14:6, and comment on the irony of Pilate's question in John 18:38, "What is truth?" given that *the* Truth was standing right in front of him in the person of Jesus.

Option 2  Chat Room

You'll need Several Bibles, pens or pencils and one copy of "Prove It" (p. 39).

Share with students that the search for truth today is not a new one, but one that has been going on for thousands of years. Distribute Bibles and have students turn to John 18:28-40. Ask for a volunteer to read the part of the narrator, another student to read the words of Pilate and a third to read the words of Christ. Everyone else is part of the crowd.

Discuss the following questions: **Who in the story could have answered Pilate's question in John 18:38?** The answer is Jesus. Point out the irony that Truth was standing right in front of Pilate and he didn't get it. **Do you think Pilate really wanted to know the answer to his question? Did the crowd want to know the truth? What keeps people from wanting to know the truth about Jesus?** The answer is basically three things: pride, ignorance and not wanting to change.

Explain: **People who don't want to know the truth about Jesus usually decide that He is a liar or a lunatic, but definitely not Lord.** Ask students to pick a partner and then distribute a copy of "Prove It" and a pen or pencil to each pair. Continue: **On this handout are a handful of Jesus' statements that were controversial and confusing to other people. The goal is to work together as a pair and pick the position of whether Jesus was a liar, lunatic or the Lord; then write a description of how each of Jesus' wild statements proves their chosen position.**

Give the pairs 10 minutes to complete this exercise. Then ask them to share their answers. Bring their attention to John 14:6 and discuss:

Do you think Jesus was just being proud when He said that He is the Truth? No, He was explaining that He was *the* true Way to God.

Option 3  Pulse Points

You'll need A pen and white board, a picture of a simple object such as a car or tree, a VCR, a TV and the video *Liar, Liar* with Jim Carrey.

Ahead of time, cue the video approximately 27 minutes from the movie's opening Universal graphic to the scene in which Carrey ends up fighting with a blue pen as he tries to lie about its color. **Please note:** Other parts of this video would be inappropriate for a junior high audience (even though many students may have seen the movie, there may be some whose parents do not allow such viewing), so you and your senior pastor and the parents will be better friends afterward if you cue the video to the exact spot.

Also ahead of time, arrange the room, or at least part of it, into a fairly tricky obstacle course by moving chairs and tables into a course that requires a student to crawl under tables, step over chairs, etc.

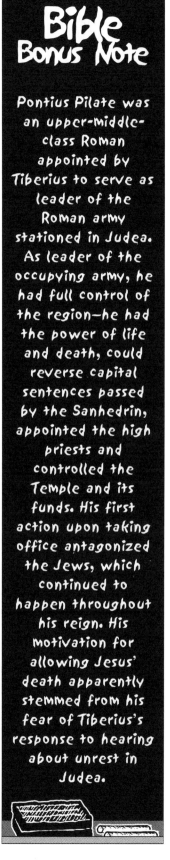

Bible Bonus Note

Pontius Pilate was an upper-middle-class Roman appointed by Tiberius to serve as leader of the Roman army stationed in Judea. As leader of the occupying army, he had full control of the region—he had the power of life and death, could reverse capital sentences passed by the Sanhedrin, appointed the high priests and controlled the Temple and its funds. His first action upon taking office antagonized the Jews, which continued to happen throughout his reign. His motivation for allowing Jesus' death apparently stemmed from his fear of Tiberius's response to hearing about unrest in Judea.

Reminder

The Big Idea

Jesus is nothing but truth.

The Big Question

How is Jesus truth?

1. Instead of being a lunatic, Jesus was the truth.

Read John 18:28-40 and explain: **The irony of Pilate's question, "What is truth?" is that *the* Truth was standing right in front of him in the person of Jesus. Everything Jesus did showed the truth, and He figured out creative ways to show the truth.**

Ask for two student volunteers. Have one student describe what the simple object in the picture looks like without naming what it is (i.e., a big circle with a line from the top to the bottom with a triangle below the circle) while another student draws the given description on the white board. Hold the picture up to the group and explain: **It's so much easier to understand what something is when it is *shown* to us instead of merely described. Although some thought Jesus was a lunatic, He was God's way of *showing* the truth to us instead of just describing it.**

2. Instead of being a liar, Jesus spoke the truth.

Show the clip from *Liar, Liar.* Explain: **No matter how much Jim Carrey's character tried, he had to speak and write the truth. The same is true with Jesus—all He could do was speak the truth** (see John 14:6;10-12).

3. As Lord, Jesus is the true way to God.

Ask for two student volunteers: one to be blindfolded and a second to lead the blindfolded volunteer through the obstacle course you have set up. Explain: **Without the sighted student showing the way through the obstacle course, the blindfolded student never would have made it. The same is true with us; we will never make it to God unless Jesus shows us the way. Other people try to make it without Jesus; but without Jesus' help, they will never find the true God, as Jesus Himself explains in John 14:6.**

STEP 3

MOVING ON

This step helps cement the idea that Jesus is the true remover of sins.

Option 1  Chat Room

You'll need A white trash bag, at least two messy liquids (i.e., ketchup, mustard, honey, Jell-o, jelly, syrup), liquid dishwashing soap in a plastic bottle and a trash can. **A low-mess alternative** for avoiding the messy liquids is to have a piece of white paper and several smaller pieces of colored construction paper (or use various colored felt-tip pens) to represent the trash bag and the messy sins.

Begin by explaining: **For the next five minutes each of us is represented by the part of the floor that we are sitting on (or the chairs we are sitting on).** Use one of the students as an example, ideally someone sitting in the center of the room who will not be embarrassed to be used as an example. Have her move out of the way and designate her previous spot on the floor as still being "her."

Explain that she's a sinner, and put the trash bag on the floor to represent her sin. Give some specific examples of her sin (i.e., mean to a little brother, cheats on tests, gossips about a friend, etc.), and each time you mention a sin, pour a messy liquid on the trash bag that represents her sin. Explain that she wants to remove the sins and tries to on her own, but that it only makes it worse. At this point, squirt dishwashing soap on the bag and rub it around, only making a bigger mess.

Continue: **The only way our sins can be removed is through Christ.** Read John 14:6 aloud and carefully roll up the trash bag, placing it and its contents in a nearby trash can as you share that Jesus is the *only* way our sins can be removed.

Option 2  Real Life

You'll need A copy of "A Letter" (p. 40), a cassette tape recorder and a blank cassette tape.

Ahead of time, ask a student volunteer to read "A Letter" and record it on cassette tape.

Begin this step by playing the cassette tape. Have students get into groups of five to seven, and discuss the last two questions: **Is the pastor right? Is the grandpa in heaven?**

Make sure that students understand that entrance to heaven comes from asking Jesus to cleanse our sins, to be our Savior and nothing else. He is the only true way to eternal life, as well as real life right now.

Option 3 Tough Questions

You'll need Just these questions.

Discuss the following:

1. **Are some truths more important than others?** Well, all truth is truth, but certainly the truth that the nearest ice cream store is three blocks away is less important than the one that Jesus removes our sins and shows us the true way to God.

2. **So are other religions following a different god?** Yes, every religion that does not believe that Christ is the true Savior is following a different god. See Exodus 20:3.

3. **Is there any truth in other religions?** Yes, truth can be learned from different religions, such as the importance of obeying your parents or our duty to help people who have less than us, but not truth about salvation and forgiveness of sins. See Acts 17:22-32.

4. **So what happens to people who have been very loyal to other religions, such as Mormonism, cults or New Age?** No matter how loyal they've been, if they haven't understood that Jesus Christ, God's Son, is the true way to God and asked Him to be their Savior, their sins are not forgiven and they are not going to heaven. See Acts 4:12; Romans 10:13.

5. **What about people before Jesus or people who have never heard of Jesus?** God holds us accountable for how we respond to information we've been given, so if people have never heard about Jesus, we can trust Him to treat them fairly.

STEP 4

MOVING OUT

This step teaches students that having Jesus as the true Savior is the only way to true happiness.

Option 1  Light the Fire

You'll need Copies of "Dear Jesus" (p. 41) and pens or pencils.

Explain: **Since we have heard the truth about Jesus as Savior, we now have the chance to respond.** Distribute copies of "Dear Jesus" and pens or pencils and ask students to be as honest as possible in writing a letter to God that explains how they are feeling about Jesus and how they want to respond to Him.

Close in prayer, asking students to pray the following words out loud if they either want to ask Jesus to be their Savior for the first time or rededicate their lives to Him:

> **Dear God, I know I'm a sinner, and I need You to forgive everything I've done. Thank You for sending Jesus to give me a way back to You. Jesus, I invite You to take control of my life and be my Savior and Lord. Thanks that I'll never be the same again. Amen.**

For students who have prayed that prayer for the first time, be sure to distribute copies of "How Can I Get to Know Jesus?" (pp. 95-96) in the back of this book.

Option 2  Fired Up

You'll need A white board and a pen, or chalkboard and chalk.

Ahead of time, ask two students to share when, why and how they asked Jesus to be their Savior. Make sure they specifically share the following three things:

- What they were like before they became Christians;
- How they became Christians;
- How their lives are different now.

To make the sharing relate to as many students as possible, it's best if one of your two students comes from a Christian background and the other student does not come from a Christian background or family.

Have the two students share their stories about asking Jesus to be their Savior. After they have finished, explain that anytime someone hears about Jesus, he or she must respond. That includes today. Write "Why?" on the board, and ask students to share the reasons

they need to ask Jesus to be their Savior. Next write "How?" on the board and explain that there is one simple way to ask Jesus to be your Savior—by praying to Him.

Close in prayer, asking students to pray the following words out loud, one phrase at a time, if they either want to ask Jesus to be their Savior for the first time or to rededicate their lives to Him:

> **Dear God, I know I'm a sinner, and I need You to forgive everything I've done. Thank You for sending Jesus to give me a way back to You. Jesus, I invite You to take control of my life and be my Savior and Lord. Thanks that I'll never be the same again. Amen.**

For students who have prayed that prayer for the first time, be sure to distribute copies of "How Can I Get to Know Jesus?" on pages 95-96 in the back of this book.

Option 3 — Spread the Fire

You'll need An adult Christian or non-Christian to prepare the following:

Ahead of time, find someone to deny that Jesus is the truth, either a non-Christian or a Christian who can play the part well. The key to this is making sure this person continues to claim that Jesus isn't the truth, but doesn't overpower the students with his or her arguments. Good examples of appropriate comments are "you go to heaven by being good" or "believing in something makes it true for you."

Begin by talking about the importance of being able to explain to others that Jesus is the truth when all of a sudden, you are interrupted by the person who is ready to debate that point. Allow the debate to unfold, and try to prompt students as much as possible to respond on their own, pointing them to the key verses of John 14:6; Romans 3:23 and Romans 6:23.

Once the guest leaves, debrief students. Find out what they think were their best answers and what they would do differently in a similar situation. Explain that these types of conversations happen all the time and use 1 Peter 3:15,16 to emphasize that we must be ready to defend our faith, but that we must always respond with gentleness and respect.

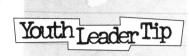

Youth Leader Tip

One of the most dangerous assumptions we make is that all of our "fired up" students are Christians. That is probably not the case. There is probably at least one junior higher who may be pretending or simply following what her friends are doing, but really hasn't made her own decision. A lesson about Christ demands we extend to junior highers the chance to ask Christ to take over their lives.

NOTES

The Liar, Lunatic or Lord Debate

Jesus' Controversial Words	Jesus as Liar	Jesus as Lunatic	Jesus as Lord
"I am The bread of life. He who comes To me will never go hungry, and he who believes in me will never be ThirsTy." John 6:35	There's no bread loaf That is big enough To feed you for your whole life.	What is Jesus—a cannibal or something? He wants us To eaT Him. ThaT's disgusting and bound To get us arrested.	Jesus knows That He is The only way To meet all of our needs, not just for food, but also for love, peace, joy and happiness.
"I am The light of The world. Whoever follows me will never walk in darkness, but will have The light of life." John 8:12	No one person can be That bright. The sun's not even That bright.	What is This guy—a human Light Bright? A plug-in flashlight? A neon glow stick? None of This is logical.	Whenever we feel like we're lost in confusion or worry, Jesus is The one To get us out of Trouble.
"I am The good shepherd. The good shepherd lays down his life for The sheep. I am The good shepherd; I know my sheep and my sheep know me—just as The FaTher knows me and I know The FaTher—and I lay down my life for The sheep." John 10:11,14,15	No shepherd cares That much about one busy sheep.	I object and I am offended. Sheep are stinky, dirty and stupid and I can't believe Jesus is referring To us as sheep.	Although iT sounds incredible, Jesus cares so much about each of us That He's willing To Trade His life for ours.
"I am The way and The TruTh and The life." John 14:6	I have my own life. No way can He claim To be The key To my life. My life is pretty cool already.	This guy is The biggest egomaniac I've ever heard of. His head must be so big That He can hardly walk into His bedroom.	There is no other way To heaven but Through Jesus ChrisT. All other paths are dead ends.
"I am The vine; you are The branches." John 15:5	I look nothing like a branch, and Jesus looks nothing like a vine in all of The pictures I've seen of Him.	This guy must be some sort of environmental freak, stuck on gardens, nature and Trees. I beT He was on drugs. Yeah, That explains some of His weird ideas.	Without Jesus, we don't have much of a life. He wants us To stay close To Him and be connected at all Times.

Prove It

Decide with your partner what you are trying to prove about who Jesus is:

He is a liar.

He is a lunatic.

He is the Lord.

Fill in the blank based on what you've decided to prove:

Our goal is to prove Jesus is _____.

Now prove your goal, using the following controversial statements made by Jesus. Next to each statement, write how this statement can be used to back up what you're trying to prove.

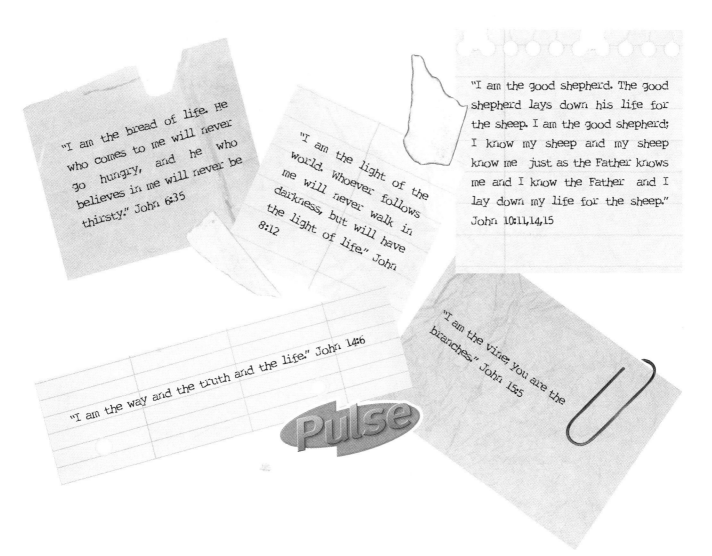

"I am the bread of life. He who comes to me will never go hungry, and he who believes in me will never be thirsty." John 6:35

"I am the light of the world. Whoever follows me will never walk in darkness, but will have the light of life." John 8:12

"I am the good shepherd. The good shepherd lays down his life for the sheep. I am the good shepherd; I know my sheep and my sheep know me just as the Father knows me and I know the Father and I lay down my life for the sheep." John 10:11,14,15

"I am the way and the truth and the life." John 14:6

Pulse

"I am the vine; you are the branches." John 15:5

A Letter

Dear

I know you're an adulT and everyThing, and This seems like someThing I need To Talk To an adulT abouT, so here goes. LasT summer my whole family flew To San Diego. IT was supposed To be a normal family vacaTion, you know, The beach and sTuff like ThaT, buT insTead my grandfaTher who lives There ended up having cancer. He looked real bad and real old. He losT a loT of weighT and goT really weak. My grandma ended up having To feed him. IT was really hard for my mom To see him. Every day when we lefT Their house, Mom would be real sad and drive away crying.

AbouT Two monThs afTer we lefT, he died. We wenT back To San Diego for The funeral, and This guy, I guess he was a pasTor, led The funeral. He kepT Talking abouT how my grandpa was forgiven and was going To be in heaven. I wanTed To believe him, buT To be honesT, I don'T Think my grandpa ever wenT To church and The only Time he ever said The name "Jesus" was as a swear word. My mom Tried To pray wiTh him on our vacaTion and he Told her, "I don'T wanT any of ThaT Jesus sTuff."

So, is The pasTor righT? Have his sins been forgiven? Is my grandpa in heaven?

Dear Jesus

Take five minutes to write a letter back to Jesus to respond to all you've learned about Him today.

Dear Jesus,

I've learned a loT about You Today, like...

Because of all I've learned and felT Today, I know ThaT I need You To...

My signaTure below shows ThaT I'm asking You To be my Savior and Take conTrol of my life.

Signed,

_____

DaTe _____

Devotions in Motion

WEEK TWO: GOD THE SON: THE LIFE

DAY 1

QUICK QUESTIONS

If you're feeling stressed, find God's answers in Matthew 6:25-34.

God Says

Read the following false statements and change the wording to make them true:

Jesus said that we have almost nothing to worry about.

Birds don't need to worry because they can fly away from any trouble.

Seek first a new bike and everything else will be given to you.

I Do

Choose two of the following areas of your life and write something down that you worry about.

School   Family   Friends   My appearance

Now pray about both of these areas, asking God to help you to stop worrying. After all, worry will only make your life a little shorter.

FOLD HERE ---

DAY 4

QUICK QUESTIONS

To read about something that only happened once in all history, read Matthew 27:62—28:10.

God Says

Why did Pilate want the guard to beef up the security at the tomb?

☐ Dead bodies had a habit of walking away in those days.

☐ The disciples might come to steal Jesus' dead body.

☐ They were afraid Jesus' body would start to stink.

How did the tomb get opened?

Pulse

Imagine you are one of the women who is running away from the tomb when all of a sudden you bump into Jesus. What would you want to say to him?

I Do

Jesus is the only person in all history who was crucified and resurrected. He could do that because he was God's Son the wants to be your best friend and take over your life, if you'll let him. Right now ask him to take over your life and help you obey him in every area of your life.

DAY 2

FAST FACTS

If you're wondering how you're going to get food today, check out Matthew 14:13-21.

God Says

You're sure the girl next to you must have heard. After all, your stomach is growling so loudly that it sounds like you swallowed a set of drums. The good thing is that your school is welcoming a new principal today, so they're feeding the whole school apple pie with vanilla ice cream. At least that should solve your hunger problem.

But when you see them bring out the pies, you know you're doomed. Only five pies for the whole school. There's no way. This is going to work. But after a few minutes, you look around and can't believe it. Even though the cafeteria workers are dishing out tons of pie with ice cream, it's not running out. The math just doesn't work here. There's got to be something else going on.

I Do

If you were hanging out with Jesus in Israel, you would know that there was definitely something going on. Just like the apple pie and ice cream, Jesus took a little bit of bread and fish and fed thousands of people. The truth is pretty simple—Jesus meets needs.

Think about an area of your life where you need something. Make sure it's really a need and not just something that you want. Ask Jesus to provide it for you. If it's His will, consider it a done deal.

FOLD HERE

DAY 3

FAST FACTS

You won't believe your eyes once you read Matthew 14:22-36.

God Says

You're sitting on the beach, hanging out with your friends and watching people water ski. Some of the water skiers are pretty good, skiing with only one ski doing twists and turns, and even skiing barefoot. But there's one guy who stands out from the rest. Not only does he not need skis, he doesn't even need a boat.

It's Jesus, and right next to Him is another guy who is trying to walk out to Him. The other guy is doing OK, but is definitely a little afraid and shaky. You think he's going to make it out to Jesus when all of a sudden he gets distracted by a nearby wave and starts to drown.

I Do

We're just like the other guy walking out toward Jesus. As long as we keep looking at Him, we do OK. When we start to look at other things, we start sinking.

Think of one area of your life where you need to see Jesus working. Ask Him to help you focus on Him and not everything else that surrounds you.

44

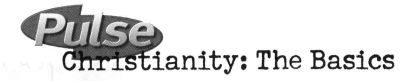

SESSIONTHREESESSIONTHREESESSIONTHREE

The Big Idea

The Holy Spirit lights the way to God.

Session Aims

In this session you will guide students to:

- Learn a key purpose of the Holy Spirit—to guide them into all truth;
- Experience the importance of being used by the Holy Spirit to show the truth to others;
- Respond by identifying ways the Holy Spirit has been active in their own lives in the past as well as ways they can be open to His lessons for them this week.

The Biggest Verse

"But when he, the Spirit of truth, comes, he will guide you into all truth." John 16:13

Other Important Verses

John 1:1,2; 14:6,16; 15:26,27; 16:5-16; Acts 9:17; 1 Corinthians 2:10; Ephesians 2:1-3; Philippians 2:8

God the Holy Spirit: The Light

STEP

MOVING IN

This step reminds students that without light, we would be in a heap of trouble.

Option 1 — Move It

You'll need A timer, two rectangular tables of equal height, four identical rectangular tablecloths (or bedsheets, at least full-bed size), a lighter, a box of matches, a light bulb, a flashlight, a candle, a lampshade, a ball approximately the size of a volleyball, several large pieces of cloth (bath towels, jackets or sweatshirts would work just fine for this) and a watch with a seconds indicator.

Ahead of time, place the rectangular tables across the front of the room the long way with approximately 10 inches between them. Lay the four tablecloths (or bedsheets) on the tables so that they look like one long table and so that the audience can't see underneath the tables at all (hence the extra cloths). Spread the lighter, matches and light bulb down the middle of the first table and the flashlight, candle and lampshade down the middle of the second table. Be sure to place the ball right on the crack between the two tables. Cover all seven objects with the pieces of cloth so that no one can see them.

> **CAUTION**
>
> To prevent this from being a very quick *and* rather traumatic game, place a wedge, a board, bricks or books between the rectangular tables to prevent an accidental "beheading by table"!

Greet students and ask for three volunteer contestants. Have the volunteers leave the room with one of the adults and go far enough away so that they can't hear what is happening in the room (somewhere between right outside the door and the donut shop down the street!). Explain that, one at a time, the contestants who are waiting outside will come in and walk along the tables, lifting one cloth at a time and shouting as quickly as possible the type of object beneath the cloth before they move to the next object and repeat the process.

But here's the trick: Remove the ball and substitute one of your most expressive and outgoing students. Have him kneel between the two tables with only his head emerging! When the contestant lifts that cloth, he will be greeted by the head of one of his friends who should shout "Hello" and startle him. Continue to urge the contestant to finish the game and name the remaining objects on the table. The key to this is to make sure that your expressive student is completely hidden by the tablecloth and the cloth over his head so it is a total surprise to the contestant. (You may need to cut a hole in one of the tablecloths/bedsheets to achieve this effect.)

One at a time, call in your contestants and explain to each that the goal is to go as quickly as possible down the table (making it seem as if it is one table), lift up one cloth at a time, shout the object under the cloth, then move ahead to the next object until finished. Tell them they will be timed.

At the end of the game, give a candle or light bulb to the contestant who finishes the fastest. Ask what all of the objects have in common, and explain that today they're going to study about the most important light ever.

Option 2 — Chat Room

You'll need The following props as visual clues for students: Iced tea, soap, lemonade, cereal, chocolate sauce, ice cream, computer disk, compact disk, phone cord, hair dye, dollar bill, T-shirt with a logo, plant, candlestick and light bulb.

Greet students, and divide them into three evenly sized groups. Give each group one of the following names: Oooo-oooo, Eeee-eeee, Aaah-aaah. Have each team practice saying its team name. Ask for two volunteers from *each* team.

Explain that you are going to read a list of three objects that have one need in common and that once you read the the list, the two volunteers need to huddle quickly to come up with a team answer; then make their team noise to get your attention. Whichever noise you hear first, ask that pair for their answer. If they are correct, award points and move to the next list of three objects and repeat the process. If their answer is wrong, ask one of the other two teams to respond. If none of the volunteers have the right answer, ask the remaining teams for their answers. Award points to the team that gets the correct answer. Some of these are hard so be prepared to give hints. Ask the members to cheer for their two volunteers by using only their team sound instead of clapping or yelling.

Here are the objects and their answers:

1. Iced tea, soap, lemonade *Answer: water.*
2. Cereal, chocolate sauce, ice cream *Answer: milk.*
3. Computer disk, compact disk, phone cord *Answer: computer.*
4. Hair dye, dollar bill, T-shirt with a logo *Answer: ink.*
5. Plant, candlestick, light bulb *Answer: light.*

When students have settled down, explain: **Any of us could have been one of the objects in the last list, because each of us needs light.** Ask: **What would happen if we didn't have light? How would today be different if there was no light? Today we're going to learn about a kind of light that is super important.**

Option 3  Fun and Games

You'll need A large damage-resistant room (or outdoor area if you don't have such a room), one inflatable beach ball (or soft Nerf-type ball) for every 10 to 15 students, four orange cones (or four chairs for the **low-tech version**), candy prizes.

Greet the group warmly and divide students into two fairly even teams. Send the two teams to opposite ends of the room and establish a goal for each team by placing the orange cones approximately eight feet apart at opposite ends of the playing area. This should look like a soccer field.

Explain that they are going to play Zany Indoor Human Foosball which is like normal soccer in that their team gets points by kicking the ball through the other team's goal—as long as the ball is no higher than the head of the goalie who is blocking the goal. It's *human* Foosball because all the players are standing spread out in even rows with alternating teams in each row facing their opponents' goal, and they can't move from that position, even as they kick the ball. Have them hold their hands behind their backs, except for the goalie. It's *indoor* because they can play off the walls and ceilings. It's *zany* because most of the game is going to be played with the lights off and because every 30 to 60 seconds, you are going to briefly turn on the lights in the room and the two students who are closest to the ball at that point must leave the game and sit on the sidelines. The team that has possession of the ball at that point gets to keep the ball and play resumes when you turn the lights off again. Play this for approximately seven minutes until nearly all the students are eliminated by the light. Award the winning team (the one with the most goals) a candy prize. Or give everyone a candy prize for being great sports.

Options: If the group is more than 40 students, try eliminating 3 or more students when the light comes on. If the room is completely dark once you turn the lights off, reverse the light/dark element and have the lights on most of the time and turn them off every 30 to 60 seconds to eliminate players.

When the game has ended, ask students: **Was the light your friend or your enemy in this game? In general, when is light something you want to stay away from?** Possible answers might be when it hurts your eyes or disturbs your sleep. **When is light something you want to hang around? Today we're going to study a light that is always our friend—in fact our best friend.**

STEP 2 — MOVING UP

This step teaches students that one of the Holy Spirit's purposes is to light up the truth about ourselves and our God.

Option 1  Move It

You'll need Several Bibles, 28 pieces of same-colored construction paper (ideally a light, bright color such as yellow, pink or light blue), pens or pencils, a section of wall (or a large bulletin board), tape (or tacks) and several felt-tip pens.

Ahead of time, write "Close—but not quite" on five pieces of construction paper and "Almost there—go again" on five pieces of construction paper.

Divide students into small groups of four to six. Make sure that each group has at least one Bible. Explain that you're going to play a game called Construction Concentration that begins with each group reading John 16:5-16 aloud, with one person in the group reading the first verse aloud, another group member reading the second verse and so on until the Scripture passage is completed.

Number off each group from 7 to 15, corresponding to John 16:7-15. (If you have more than nine groups, some groups will receive the same number; fewer than nine groups means some groups will receive more than one number.) Take the number of verses assigned to each group and multiply that by two and give that amount of construction paper to each group along with a pen. For example, a group with one verse will get two pieces of paper, another group with two verses will get four pieces, etc.

Ask each group to summarize in fewer than seven words the characteristic of the Holy Spirit that Jesus describes in their assigned verse and write their summary on both pieces of construction paper.

Collect the papers and combine them with the 10 that you prepared ahead of time, making sure to mix them up. Tape (or tack) the papers in rows and columns to a wall (or bulletin board) with the writing *facing the wall*. Number the backsides of the papers to avoid the momentum-killing-inevitably-boring instructions from students "No, not that one...higher...a little lower...a bit to the right...the one below that."

Ask for a volunteer from each team to choose two pieces of paper to turn over in search of a match. If they get the match, they get to guess again. Continue asking for volunteers from both teams until every characteristic has been matched with its identical partner.

Suggestion: To reinforce the characteristics of the Holy Spirit, collect all the papers once the game is over and ask students to share phrases that they remember. Ask which group had verse 13, and have them read that verse aloud. Explain that verse 13 is the best summary for all of the other characteristics of the Holy Spirit because the Holy Spirit is the One who lights up the truth for us.

Option 2  Chat Room

You'll need Several Bibles, copies of "Name That Job" (p. 53) and pens or pencils.

Distribute pens or pencils and copies of "Name That Job" to students and ask them to work in pairs to complete the questions. Once they have finished, give each pair a Bible and ask them to look up John 16:5-16 to see if this text changes any of their answers.

When students have finished changing their answers to match John 16, ask for volunteers to share their answers. The correct answers are as follows (you may want to have students look up the corresponding Scripture verses):

1. The Savior Son—Philippians 2:8
2. The Helpful Holy Spirit—1 Corinthians 2:10
3. The Helpful Holy Spirit—John 14:16
4. The Savior Son—John 14:6
5. The Helpful Holy Spirit—John 16:13
6. The Savior Son—John 1:1,2
7. The Savior Son—Philippians 2:8
8. The Helpful Holy Spirit—Acts 9:17
9. The Savior Son—John 14:6
10. The Helpful Holy Spirit—John 16:7

Be sure to explain that some of the answers, especially numbers 6 and 9, could easily be both the Savior Son and the Helpful Holy Spirit. Then ask:

What were the easiest answers to come up with?

What were the hardest? What is one new thing that you have learned?

If you had to explain the job of Christ to a six-year-old, what would you say?

How would you describe the Holy Spirit's job?

Explain the importance of the Holy Spirit as our guide into the truth (see John 16:13). Point out the interesting and ironic truth that we need the Holy Spirit to help us understand the Holy Spirit; our own brains just can't get it on their own.

Option 3  Pulse Points

You'll need Music (either from a worship team or a CD player), three pieces of paper, a felt-tip pen, three candy bars and transparent tape.

Ahead of time, write the following on three different pieces of paper: "Whatever God wants to tell me is what I tell you," "If you need to know the truth, just ask me" and "Here's one truth that's for sure: God loves you so much that He sent Christ to die for you." Tape one of the pieces of paper to each of the three candy bars.

The Big Idea

A key purpose of the Holy Spirit is to guide us into the truth.

The Big Question

How does the Holy Spirit guide us into truth?

1. He is a sin convicter—
John 16:5-12

Ask students to share their favorite childhood game. Explain that one game you liked was Duck-Duck-Goose. (**Note:** If that's not true, don't lie, but explain that one game you remember is Duck-Duck-Goose. Unless that's not true; in that case you are on your own to transition to Duck-Duck-Goose and how to play it!)

Explain: **When God sees an area of your life that needs correcting, He uses the conviction of the Holy Spirit. This conviction always comes out of God's love for us and His desire to keep us on the right path. We need the Holy Spirit to point out the areas in our lives that are offtrack with God's purpose. His conviction allows us to repent and get right with God. Conviction never condemns us or lays a deep sense of guilt upon us. That's called condemnation and _it_ comes from the enemy. Condemnation is meant to distance us from the Lord through feelings of worthlessness and despair. With this in mind, think about the game Duck-Duck-Goose. The Holy Spirit is like the person who is "It" in the game except He taps every single person on the shoulder and says the same thing: "Sinner."** If you have time, tap three to five students on their shoulders and say "Sinner" for dramatic effect.

2. He is a speaker of God—
John 16:13-16

Ask a student of your same gender to come forward and designate that student as "the Holy Spirit" and yourself as "God." Once students' giggles over the idea of you being God subside, explain that the Holy Spirit says exactly what God says to Him. Explain that the Holy Spirit's messages are on these three pieces of paper and that the "Holy Spirit" (a.k.a. the student volunteer) is going to throw the messages (which happen to be attached to candy bars) to three different students. Ask each of the three students who catch the candy bars to read the messages from the Holy Spirit aloud.

STEP 3 — MOVING ON

The goal of this step is to help students identify ways the Holy Spirit has been active in their own lives.

Option 1  Chat Room

You'll need A copy of a sensational tabloid newspaper (_The National Enquirer,_ for example) and a copy of a more serious newspaper with today's date.

Start the group chat by opening the sensational newspaper and pointing out some of the humorous and ludicrous titles. (**Note:** It's best to skim through it ahead of time and pick a few titles to avoid one of those oh-no-I'm-going-to-hear-from-parents-about-this moments.) Then, using the first few pages of today's more serious newspaper, ask for volunteers to come up and close their eyes and point randomly to an article on the page. Read the headline for that article and discuss the following questions:

Given what we know about the way the Holy Spirit lights up the truth for people, how might the Holy Spirit have been involved in this story?

How might the Holy Spirit intend to show the truth to people in this story in the future?

Divide students into small groups of four to six, and ask them to think about their lives this past week. Ask them to share in groups: **If you had to write a headline that summarized something that happened in your life, what would it be?** Then ask the groups to brainstorm how the Holy Spirit might have been involved in that headline. This might be a developmental stretch for the expanding minds of your junior highers, so be prepared to give a few examples: a time when He helped you learn what you needed to pass a math test or when He gave you the right words to help lift the spirit of a depressed friend.

After giving the groups five minutes to share, bring students back together and discuss: **Can we block what the Holy Spirit intends to do?** Turn off the lights in your room and explain that we can, in fact, hinder lessons the Holy Spirit is trying to teach us. While the lights are still off, ask: **What can we do to be more open to the light the Holy Spirit is trying to show us?**

Option 2  Real Life

You'll need Paper and pencils.

Ask students how much time they spend online with their computers. Ask them to imagine that they've received the following E-mail and need to respond:

> I'm not sure if you are going to be able to help me with my problem, but anyway, here it is. My name is Becky, and I've been going to church for three or four years now. I started going because my best friend, Susan, invited me to a movie night and I've been going ever since, mostly because of the fun games and the guys I've met.
>
> Well, since I've started going to church, my older brother decided to come also. He's in college and is pretty smart. It's pretty cool because he can drive me to church, and I don't always have to ask my mom to take me.
>
> He goes to church all the time now. Prayer meetings, church services, missions meetings, game nights—you name it; just about anytime the doors are open, my brother Matt is there.
>
> And all he talks about now is church, not so much to my dad because he doesn't want to hear about it, but mostly to my mom and me. Most of what he says sounds sort of familiar, like about God's love and His Son Jesus and all that. But this last week Matt's been talking a lot about the Holy Spirit, and I have no idea what he means. I feel stupid because I've been going to church longer than he has, so I don't want to ask him. I've read about God and Jesus in the Bible, but what is this Holy Spirit thing all about? Brian keeps talking about all the Holy Spirit is doing in his life. What's he mean by that? If you know, maybe you could E-mail me back to let me know stuff this Holy Spirit has done in your life.

Ask students to form groups of four each and give each group a piece of paper and a pencil. Ask the student with the longest hair in each group to write the first sentence of an answer that explains about the Holy Spirit to Becky. When that student finishes the first sentence, she passes the paper and pencil to the next student who writes the next sentence, and so on until the group has finished the E-mail answer.

Ask groups to read their E-mails aloud. If they didn't get specific enough about ways the Holy Spirit has shown them the truth in their own lives, ask them follow-up questions to help them be more specific.

Option 3  Tough Questions

You'll need The following questions.

For students who love to wrestle with the bigger and tougher questions about the Holy Spirit, lead the following discussion:

1. **Aren't God the Father and Jesus enough?** Yes and no. They are enough, but one of the ways they provide for all of our needs, including our need for truth, is through the Holy Spirit.
2. **Is God more powerful than the Holy Spirit?** No, they are equal in power but different in purpose.
3. **When did the Holy Spirit start acting in the world?** The Holy Spirit has been present and active since the world was created, but it wasn't until Jesus was resurrected that He started living inside believers.
4. **When does the Holy Spirit become active in a Christian's life?** At the moment that person asks Jesus to be his or her Savior and Lord.
5. **What do I have to do to receive the Holy Spirit?** You get the Holy Spirit in your life once you ask Jesus to take control of your life and be your Savior.
6. **Do I have to speak in tongues to be filled with the Holy Spirit?** No, the Holy Spirit enters our lives when we come to know Christ as Savior. The gift of speaking in tongues can be evidence of the indwelling of the Holy Spirit, but not all Christians have that particular gift.

NOTES

STEP 4
MOVING OUT

This step helps students identify one or more areas in their lives where they want to be open to new lessons from the Holy Spirit.

Option 1  Light the Fire

You'll need A Bible, 3x5-inch index cards, pens or pencils, tape, a mirror, a schoolbook, a phone (unplugged would probably be easier since it's tough to find cords that will stretch from your house or office to your meeting place!), a picture of you with your friends (or a magazine picture representing the same thing), a picture of you with your family (or a magazine picture) and window cleaner or a dust rag.

Ahead of time, place everything (except the index cards, pens and tape) in a large paper bag or box with a lid. Explain that the Holy Spirit is trying to light up new truths about ourselves and God in every area of our lives. One object at a time, pull out the mirror, the Bible, the book, the phone, the picture of friends, the picture of family and the window cleaner or dust rag. As you pull each item out of the bag or box, ask students what area of their lives that object represents. The answers should be:

Mirror = self-image
Bible = relationship with God
Book = school
Phone = pastimes/activities
Photo of you with your friends = friends
Photo of you with your family = family
Window cleaner or a dust rag = chores

Place each of these seven objects at various locations around the room. Ask students to choose one of these areas in which they believe that God, through the Holy Spirit, is already trying to teach them a new truth and go stand by the object that represents that area. Give an index card and pen or pencil to each student. While the students are still near their chosen objects, have them write their names and what they think the Holy Spirit is trying to teach them on the cards. Have them exchange cards with another student who is standing by the same

object and ask them to commit to praying for each other *at least* twice during the next week.

Close the session by walking around the room, going to each object and praying briefly for the students standing near that object and for their openness to the truth the Holy Spirit intends to teach them.

Option 2  Fired Up

You'll need Pens or pencils and copies of "Prayer Pairs" (p. 54).

This prayer-pair exercise is a great, tangible opportunity for students who are already hungry to be changed by the Holy Spirit. Distribute a pen or pencil and a copy of "Prayer Pairs" to each person. Explain that this calendar is geared to help us pray for each other every day for the next week. Once students have completed their "Prayer Pairs" sheets, have them pair up and exchange prayer sheets as a daily reminder of how to pray specifically for each other during the next seven days. If there is time, allow pairs to pray right then and there.

Option 3  Spread the Fire

You'll need Your Bible, one large candle and a book of matches.

Ask for a volunteer to read John 15:26,27 aloud and ask if any student can summarize the verse in his or her own words, applying Jesus' words to His original disciples to those of us who are His disciples today, almost 2,000 years later. The summary should resemble something like this: "God sends the Holy Spirit to share the truth about Himself, and He wants us to tell others about Him also."

Light the candle and explain that you are going to name someone that you want to see the Holy Spirit show the truth about God. Once you say that name aloud, the rest of the group should pray silently for the person you named while you move to another student and hand that student the candle. That student then says someone's name aloud, triggering the rest of the students to pray silently for that student, while the candle is handed to another. This should continue for a few minutes or until every student has had the chance to say a friend's name aloud and the group has prayed for that friend.

Name That Job

Decide whether this is the job of Jesus or the Holy Spirit. Write your answer in the outer circle.

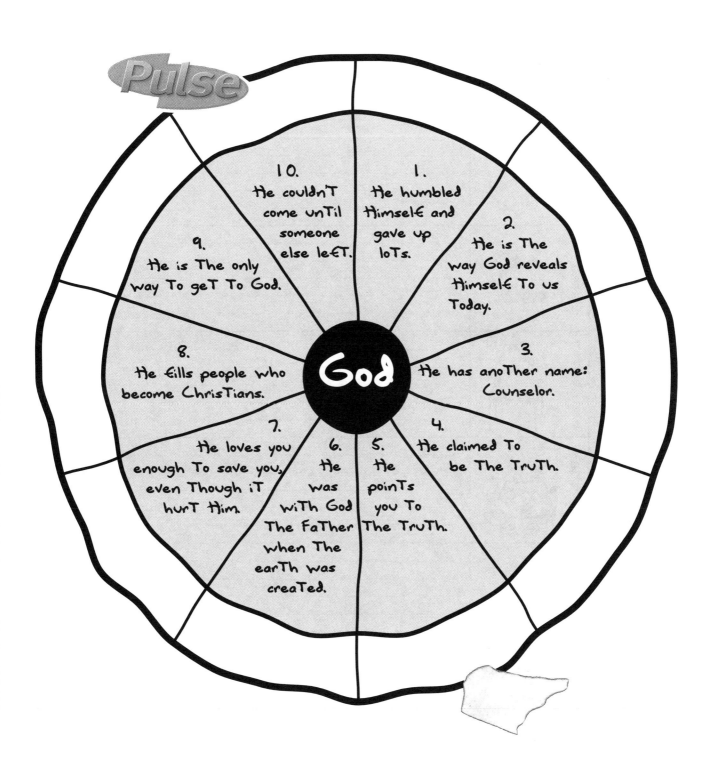

God

1. He humbled Himself and gave up loTs.

2. He is The way God reveals Himself To us Today.

3. He has anoTher name: Counselor.

4. He claimed To be The TruTh.

5. He poinTs you To The TruTh.

6. He was wiTh God The FaTher when The earTh was creaTed.

7. He loves you enough To save you, even Though iT hurT Him.

8. He fills people who become ChrisTians.

9. He is The only way To geT To God.

10. He couldn'T come unTil someone else lefT.

Pulse

Prayer Pairs

First, try to figure out what each of the pictures in each day symbolizes. Once you've done that, complete the calendar by writing in each box at least one way you think the Holy Spirit is trying to light up a truth in that area. For example, once you figure out what the picture for Sunday means, jot down in Sunday's box one lesson you think the Holy Spirit is trying to teach you about that area of your life.

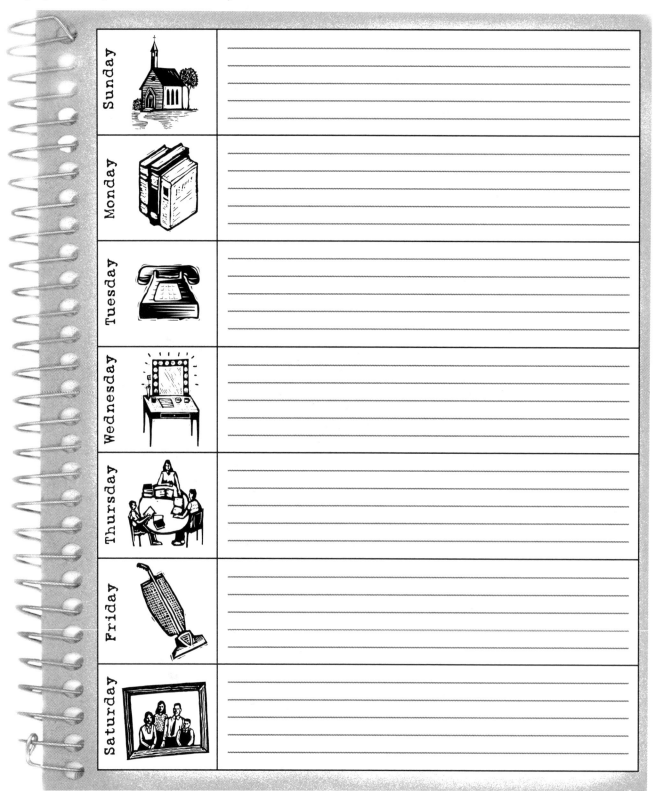

Devotions in Motion

WEEK THREE: GOD THE HOLY SPIRIT:
THE LIGHT

DAY 1

QUICK QUESTIONS

Check out what God said a long time ago in Isaiah 63:7-10:

God Says

What are some of the "good things" God has done for His people?

- ☐ Free popcorn and soft drinks at every movie.
- ☐ Peace and joy when we need it.
- ☐ Straight A's in all of our classes, even in math.
- ☐ A permanent "I never ever have to do chores again" excuse.
- ☐ Salvation through Jesus Christ.
- ☐ The chance to read all about Him in The Bible.

What happens to the Holy Spirit when we sin?

It's pretty harsh to think of the Holy Spirit as the enemy of people who rebel. Why do you think the Holy Spirit hates it so much when we disobey?

I Do

Think of one word that describes how the Holy Spirit feels about how you have been acting this last week.

What is one thing that you did last week that you should repent of right now?

FOLD HERE -

DAY 4

FAST FACTS

Find Ephesians 1:11-14, and see how Paul's words relate to your life.

God Says

Now you probably send most of your mail over your computer through E-mail but every once in a while you might send a letter to a friend through the post office. Right before you plop it in the mailbox, what do you do? You lick the envelope to close it up. This seals it, and the letter inside it is now safe.

That's what happens to us once we ask Jesus to take control of our lives. He seals us with the Holy Spirit, meaning that we can feel secure because He is in control. We're protected by this presence and peace (that's presence and peace, not presents and peas), not only while we're alive now but also when we die and go to heaven.

I Do

What is the biggest thing you are worrying about today? Remember that you are sealed and surrounded by the Holy Spirit and that He will take care of you. How does this make you feel differently about what you are going through? Makes you feel better, doesn't it?

FAST FACTS

Open your Bible to Romans 8:26,27 and dive into the following.

God Says

You're stumped. Your best friend, Robyn, called you last night crying. "They're at it again," she said, "I just wish my parents would stop fighting. I think they're going to get a divorce soon and I don't know what to do about it." Your mind went blank and the only thing you could think to mumble was, "I'll pray for you, I guess." But now you have NO idea how to pray for her or what to pray about.

But the Holy Spirit does. You simply ask, "Holy Spirit, please show me what to pray for." And the Holy Spirit does. Before you go to bed, the Holy Spirit shows you that you should ask God to give Robyn peace and to bring her parents back together.

I Do

Think of the toughest thing going on in your life, or maybe a friend's life. It may even have you stumped about how to pray for it. Right now ask the Holy Spirit to guide you and show you how to pray.

FOLD HERE --

QUICK QUESTIONS

Hey, flip open your Bible and see what Paul wrote to the people who lived in this town called Corinth in 1 Corinthians 6:1 8-20.

God Says

Paul makes a pretty big deal about sexual sins. How are they different from other sins?

Right at this very moment, where is the Holy Spirit living?

I Do

Think of your favorite TV show. How would Paul describe it?

- ☐ Squeaky clean
- ☐ A little stained
- ☐ Pretty muddy
- ☐ Black and filthy

Who is one adult you can go to if you have questions on need someone's help about being sexually pure?

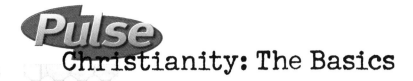
SessionFourSessionFourSessionFourSessionFour

The Big Idea

Sin is not just what we do—it's part of who we are, and it makes us guilty before God.

Session Aims

In this session you will guide students to:

- Know that they are completely contaminated by sin, a sin that is so deep that they can't remove it on their own;
- Experience the need to confess their sins to God and each other;
- Respond by being honest with themselves, God and others about the ways they've sinned during the last week.

The Biggest Verse

"All of us also lived among them at one time, gratifying the cravings of our sinful nature and following its desires and thoughts. Like the rest, we were by nature objects of wrath." Ephesians 2:3

Other Important Verses

Psalm 51:5; 103:12; Matthew 5:27,28; Acts 7:54—8:1; Romans 3:23; 4:6-8; James 5:16; 1 John 1:9,10

Our Condition: Guilty

STEP

MOVING IN

This step establishes the definition of sin as falling short of God's design.

Option 1  Move It

You'll need One 12-inch piece of rope (at least one-half inch in diameter, with a knot at each end) per student, one large trash can for every 10 students, rowdy music and a prize for the winner (a small trash can would be appropriate).

Greet students warmly and ask them if they are ready to dive into a wild Trash-Can Slam activity. Divide students into groups of 10—separating by gender and size is a good idea to prevent injury—and have each group make a circle around a trash can. Hand each student a piece of rope and explain that they are to hold one end of the rope and offer their neighbor the other end of the rope, thereby creating a circle alternating bodies and ropes around the trash can. Explain that the goal is to avoid the trash can as long as possible while everyone else around the circle is pulling, yanking and twisting on their ropes in an effort to try to slam each other into the trash can. If anyone gets pulled into the trash can, even just lightly grazing it, or if anyone lets go of the rope, they are out. Play rowdy music and let the Trash-Can Slam circles continue until only one contestant is left in each circle. Bring those winners together around one trash can and play one championship round. Give the winner a trash can as a prize.

> **Options:** If you have a limited playing area, limited equipment and/or a very large group, you may have to rotate groups of players. Also, if you have only two people left and they seem to be of equal strength (i.e., neither one is going to give up), you may have to declare a tie to avoid "a duel to the death."

Ask the winner: **What was your secret strategy?** Then ask students who were eliminated early: **What was hard about the game?** Explain: **Often in life we feel like we**

are being pulled and yanked because of the sin that is inside us. We do things that we know are wrong even when we don't want to. Sin can be defined as falling short of God's design. Just like in this game, no matter how hard we try, we'll eventually fall short of God's design. Read Romans 3:23 aloud as confirmation of this definition of sin.

Option 2 Chat Room

You'll need Two boxes of Cocoa Puffs cereal, a piece of rope approximately five feet long and a box of tissues!

Greet students with enthusiasm and then ask for three volunteers for a new game called The Cocoa Puffs Snort. Explain that they are to press one finger against one nostril to close it off while *lightly* sticking a Cocoa Puff in the remaining nostril *as carefully as possible*. Then they blow and let the cereal fly. (This is where the tissue might come in handy!)

> ⚠CAUTION
> The key to avoiding ambulance rides to the hospital and the difficult conversation with parents trying to explain why you had their child stick a piece of cereal up his or her nose is to *barely* stick it in the nostril.

First, get two other student volunteers to stand one foot away from your three contestants and hold a rope about four feet from the ground; then give the contestants three chances to make it over the rope "for height." Second, lay the rope in a circle with an 18-inch diameter about two feet away from your three contestants and give them three chances to snort a Cocoa Puff into the circle "for accuracy." Finally, lay the rope an absurd distance away from the contestants—we suggest at least eight feet—and give them three chances to snort a Cocoa Puff across the rope "for distance." Give a prize (what else would seem fitting but a complimentary box of Cocoa Puffs) to the winning snorter.

Ask all three contestants:

What was the hardest goal to reach: height, accuracy or distance? The answer should be distance. Explain that it's frustrating when we fall short of a goal.

What other goals do we tend to fall short of? Share that there's one goal we fall short of every day, and that's the goal of God's design for us. There's a word for that: "sin."

How would you define "sin"? Sin means falling short of God's plan for us, and it's something we do all the time. Read Romans 3:23 aloud as proof of this definition of sin.

Option 3  Fun and Games

You'll need A bedsheet, a plastic tarp, several small pieces of red, yellow, green and blue construction paper placed in a box, basket or paper bag, 20 aluminum pie pans, *strawberry* jelly, a dozen eggs (beaten in a bowl), *green* peas and *blue* Jell-O.

Ahead of time, lay out the plastic tarp, then place 20 pie pans in four rows of five on top of the tarp, with approximately 12 inches between each pan. Fill one row of five pans with the jelly, one row with the eggs (preferably beaten), one row with green peas and one row with blue Jell-O. Make sure to lay the pie pans out in a place that is central and visible in room; then cover them with a bedsheet.

Greet students and explain: **Today we're going to play a new game called Terrible Twister.** Ask for four volunteers, and have them remove their socks and shoes as you remove the sheet that is covering the pie pans. Explain that you are going to ask the audience to shout out one of the following commands: left foot, right foot, left hand or right hand while you simultaneously pick a color of paper. Each contestant must then put that body part in a pie pan with that color. The contestants must first reach and stretch for unoccupied pie pans and although they can never put more than one of their own hands or feet in the same pie pan, they can share pie pans with another contestant once all of the pie pans of a certain color are occupied. Once a contestant falls, he or she is out; but in the meantime you'll have the funny opportunity to watch your four students ankle deep in blue Jell-O and green peas while madly reaching for red jelly and yellow eggs.

Ask the willing volunteers to clean up as you explain: **The goal of this game was not to fall down.** Ask students to share times when they have fallen down, such as while skateboarding or bike riding—you should also be prepared to share a story. Continue: **We actually fall every day because every day we fall short of God's design for us. That's what "sin" is: falling short of God's plan for us and that's what we will be studying today.** Read Romans 3:23 as a summary of this definition of sin.

This step helps students understand that our sin contaminates everything about us.

Option 1  Move It

You'll need A squirt gun, a white board and marker.

Have a volunteer read Ephesians 2:1-3. Ask students to pay attention to keywords while you read the passage a second time. Write down the keywords on the white board as students share them.

Explain: **By our nature, we are sinful—we want to do our own thing instead of doing what God wants us to do. Just like we can't change the fact that we're human, or that we're male or female, we can't change the fact that we're sinners. Our sin contaminates everything we do. As a result, we miss out on His best for us.**

Call on one of your most outgoing and dramatic students and have him or her come to the front of the room. Explain that you're going to test what activities are likely to cause us to sin. Give the student the task of acting out something she tends to do after school, such as eating or talking on the phone. Explain that once you squirt her with a squirt gun, she then needs to keep doing that activity, but sin while she's doing it. For example, she may refuse to share her snack with her sister or gossip while she's on the phone. After 15 seconds of her acting, squirt her with the squirt gun and see what kind of sin she can incorporate into her activity.

Ask for another student volunteer to act something out, but this time have the audience give ideas for the volunteer to pretend to be doing. Encourage the audience to come up with random, creative tasks that make it more challenging for the student actor to come up with a way to sin.

Read Ephesians 2:1-3 again. Continue: **Did this activity prove or disprove what Paul says in the passage about how deeply contaminated we are by sin? It's important to clarify that our *sins* (note the plural) are the wrong actions that are caused by our *sin* (note the singular), meaning our corrupted nature.**

Option 2  Chat Room

You'll need Several Bibles, copies of "Common Comments" (p. 64), pens or pencils, a TV, a VCR and the video *The Empire Strikes Back*.

Ahead of time, cue the video approximately one hour and 42 minutes from the opening Twentieth Century Fox graphic, where Luke Skywalker and Darth Vader are battling and Luke is tempted to give in to the "dark side."

Ask students to find a partner, ideally someone they don't know very well. Distribute a pen or pencil and a copy of "Common Comments" to each pair and give them five minutes to write down everything they have in common. Their comments should avoid the obvious things—such as having two eyes, both are girls or both breathe—and should focus on more unique qualities, such as both listen to the same radio station, both slept through their alarm today or both have pet snakes. After five minutes, ask the partners to share with the whole group a few of the most unique or wild qualities they have in common.

Explain that there's one more thing that they have in common because all people share it—we're all sinners. Next, play *The Empire Strikes Back* video clip.

Distribute Bibles and ask for a student volunteer to read Ephesians 2:1-3. Discuss the following questions:

What was similar in what Luke Skywalker and Darth Vader were talking about and Ephesians 2:1-3? Both show that sin is deep inside us, that it wants to rule us and that we are often tempted to give into sinful desires like anger or hatred.

What does it mean to be "dead" in our sins? It means having no ability to not sin, just as when our bodies are physically dead, they are unable to do anything.

Who is the "ruler of the kingdom of the air" in verse 2? Satan.

How does he fit in with sin? He encourages it.

Give an example of what it means to "gratify our cravings."

Is there anything we can do to avoid being "objects of wrath"? No, Ephesians 2:3 teaches that we are objects of wrath by our nature.

Option 3  Pulse Points

You'll need The video *The Empire Strikes Back*, something that has died (i.e., dried flowers, a dead plant or a leather jacket) and a bag of potato chips.

Ahead of time, cue the video approximately one hour and 42 minutes from the opening Twentieth Century Fox graphic, where Luke Skywalker and Darth Vader are battling and Luke is tempted to give in to the "dark side."

The Big Idea
Our sin contaminates everything about us.

The Big Question
What does sin do to us?

1. Sin kills us.
Read Ephesians 2:1. Explain that just like the "dead" prop, sin makes us feel dead and robs us of joy, peace and life itself.

2. Sin calls us.
Read Ephesians 2:2 and share how evil is inside of us, always calling. Play *The Empire Strikes Back* clip and explain how Luke Skywalker felt the evil and anger building inside of him and that he was tempted to give in to the dark side.

3. Sin compels us.
Read Ephesians 2:3 and share that once we start gratifying our sinful desires, it's hard to stop. Give each student one potato chip, and then ask if they would like another one. The obvious answer is yes, since it's almost impossible to eat just one chip. Explain that this is how we feel when we sin—the more we do it, the more we want to keep on doing it.

This step shows students that our sin is so deep that we can't remove it on our own.

Option 1  Chat Room

You'll need Several Bibles.

Ask: **If you knew you had had three minutes before you were going to die and you had the chance to give a speech, what would you say?** Explain that there's an example of someone who knew he was going to die and said some powerful things right before he was killed. Distribute Bibles and ask for a volunteer to read Acts 7:54—8:1. Discuss:

Why do you think the people around Stephen "covered their ears" during his last words as he started talking about heaven?

How would you describe Stephen's attitude toward the people who were killing him?

Explain: **In this story we meet Saul, later known as Paul, one of the people who wrote about how deep our sins are. How is Stephen's attitude toward Saul different than Saul's attitude toward Stephen?**

Ask: **This is the first time we read about Saul in Scripture, but if you had to summarize what he's like using three different words, what would they be?**

Continue: **Saul went on to become a Christian, changed his name to Paul and wrote more books of the Bible than any other person, but he sure started as a major sinner. Saul was the one who approved of Stephen's death—is there anything he could have done to remove his sin afterward?** He could only ask Christ to forgive him. **The same is true for us; even when we've done mean things, there's nothing we can do to get rid of feeling guilty about it, except ask Christ to forgive us.**

Option 2  Real Life

You'll need Your Bible, a newspaper, white board and pen.

Ahead of time, find a story (either in the national or local news) in which someone is accused of doing something wrong.

Quickly explain that you've brought a newspaper today because one story interested you so much that you wanted to share it with everyone. Read a few paragraphs from the story and then ask students to imagine that they have just been asked to be the prosecuting attorney to argue that this person is guilty and should go to jail. The defense attorney in the case, who opposes them, is arguing that the accused will become nicer as time goes by. Add that the judge is a Christian and seems open to adding some scripture to the argument. Remind the students of Ephesians 2:1-3 and Romans 3:23, and ask them to share some of their ideas for arguments as you write their answers on the white board. Discuss:

What were some of the common themes in the arguments? How is the Bible important evidence for our argument? Share that the accused person could be any of us because, although we may not have murdered someone or stolen something, we have done some things that were totally wrong.

Option 3  Tough Questions

You'll need Your Bible and a sharp mind to handle these questions.

1. **How did sin start?** It began in the Garden of Eden when Adam and Eve rebelled against God.
2. **Why does God allow people to sin?** Just as He lets people choose to love Him, He also lets people choose not to love Him. He doesn't want us to be robots who have to serve Him, but people who decide to serve Him.
3. **Are people by nature good or evil?** We are good in the sense that we are created by God, but evil in the sense that we are totally contaminated by our sin.
4. **What's worse: sin in our thoughts or sin in our actions?** They're both equally wrong. Jesus condemned sin in our thoughts in Matthew 5:27,28, but sin in our actions is also condemned.
5. **Is there any such thing as a sinless action?** No, sin contaminates everything about us, including our every action. Even when we do something "good" to help people, we can be motivated by wanting them to like us or hoping they'll do something in return.
6. **How can we get into heaven if we're all sinners?** That's the amazing thing about it! Even though we're all sinners, God loves us so much that He gave us a way to get into heaven; all we have to do is ask Jesus to take over our lives.
7. **How can little babies be sinful like it says in Psalm 51:5?** Because we're all humans descended from Adam and Eve, we all inherited their sin—even cute little babies.

NOTES

STEP 4

MOVING OUT

This step shows students the importance of being honest about their sins with themselves, with God and with each other.

Option 1 — Light the Fire

You'll need Several Bibles, copies of "Sure, I'm a Sinner" (p. 65) and pens or pencils.

Remind students that all of us are sinners. Take a few minutes to share one area in your own life in which you still struggle with sin. As you share about yourself, make sure you are sincere and vulnerable without "emotionally vomiting" all over your students.

Distribute copies of "Sure, I'm a Sinner" and pens or pencils to students. Ask them to complete the sentence, "Dear God, I know I'm a sinner. I am sorry that I sin in the area of…" on their papers. Then have students bring the papers forward and lay them facedown at the front of the room. Read 1 John 1:9,10 and explain how wonderful it is that we have a God who forgives our sins. Rip up all of the "Sure, I'm a Sinner" papers and throw them in the trash; then read Psalm 103:12, thanking God in prayer for the way He forgives and forgets our sin.

Option 2 — Fired Up

You'll need Several Bibles.

Ask for a volunteer to read 1 John 1:9,10 and another volunteer to read James 5:16. Explain that in the midst of our sin, God wants us to confess what we've done to Him and to each other. The good news is that He is faithful and just and will forgive us for our sin.

Instruct students to find one or two other people and take some time to confess their sins to each other, then to God in prayer. **Note:** Be sure to stress the importance of confidentiality. Allow enough time for everyone to complete their confessions and, when everyone is done, read

Psalm 103:12 and Romans 4:6-8. Remind students that once we confess our sins, God doesn't count them against us anymore.

Option 3 — Spread the Fire

You'll need Two copies of "Perfect Paula" (p. 66).

Ahead of time, give "Perfect Paula" to two students to practice and memorize ahead of time. It's best if Paula is wearing a Christian T-shirt and carrying her Bible, as well as any other props you think of that scream "I'm a Christian."

Ask the two student actors to come forward and perform the drama. Share that Paula's advice to Candice didn't work out like she hoped it would. Non-Christians don't want to hear about how perfect our lives are because they're not. They want to hear about our struggles and how Jesus helps us in the midst of our problems.

Ask students to brainstorm things that Paula could have said or done that would have made her advice more effective. Ask them to each pray for one specific friend and that they would have the chance to talk with their friends this week about how Jesus helps them in the midst of their temptations or problems.

NOTES

Common Comments

With your partner, make a list of things that the two of you have in common. You can check out the margins of this sheet for ideas.

Sports, Family Members, Pets, Television Shows, Radio Stations, Music, Favorite Foods, Favorite Colors, Places Visited, Best Subject in School, Future Dreams,

Sure, I'm a Sinner

Dear God,

I know I'm a sinner. Help me To change in This area of sin...

Dear God,

I know I'm a sinner. Help me To change in This area of sin...

Dear God,

I know I'm a sinner. Help me To change in This area of sin...

Christianity: The Basics

Perfect Paula

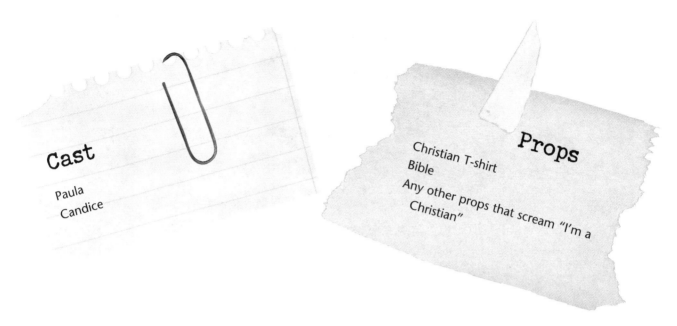

Cast

Paula
Candice

Props

Christian T-shirt
Bible
Any other props that scream "I'm a Christian"

Paula and Candice enter the room. Paula is wearing or carrying all of the Christian props.

Paula: Wow, I am so glad that our math test is over. That was really hard. I think I blew it on that last part.

Candice: Yeah, me too. It looks like partial credit is my only hope now.

Paula: Well, anyway, now we can get ready for basketball practice.

Candice: *(Pauses and looks confused.)* Hey Paula, can I ask you something?

Paula: Sure, what?

Candice: Well, I was sort of looking around class during our test and I noticed Matt and Linda sitting next to you. I don't know if you saw, but everytime Mrs. Wellman turned around, they would slip papers back and forth.

Paula: Yeah, I saw. More than that, they asked me before class if I wanted to see the papers, too.

Candice: What were the papers?

Paula: They were answers to last year's test. Matt and Linda heard that Mrs. Wellman's tests are the same every year, and since Matt's older sister had Mrs. Wellman, he found her old tests and passed them back and forth to Linda the whole time.

Candice: Do you think it helped them?

Paula: I heard them giggling afterwards about how easy the test was, so I'm guessing that the questions were the same as last year.

Candice: If you knew all this, why didn't you want to see the papers?

Paula: *(Becoming a little too friendly and enthusiastically pointing to her Christian T-shirt.)* Candice, I'm so glad you asked. See, I'm a Christian, and I believe that cheating is a sin and is wrong and therefore I don't do it.

Candice: But didn't you want to?

Paula: *(Hesitating as if trying to figure out the right thing to say.)* Oh no, Candice, like I said, cheating is wrong, so I never want to do it.

Candice: You mean you're never tempted to do the wrong thing?

Paula: Nope, like I said before, I'm a Christian. I don't sin.

Candice: *(Shaking head.)* I just can't be that perfect. I would have totally asked Matt and Linda to see the papers if I had known. There's no way that I'll *never* want to cheat. So I guess I can never be a Christian.

Devotions in Motion

WEEK FOUR: OUR CONDITION: GUILTY

DAY 1

FAST FACTS

Grab That Bible of yours and check out Psalm 51:5.

God Says

It's bad enough That you're babysitting on a Friday night instead of spending the night at Maria's house. But the way the Three-year-old you're watching is acting is making it way, way worse. He's Throwing a Tantrum, not To mention The fact That he's Throwing everything he can get his hands on. From chucking stuffed animals To hurling soup spoons To launching blocks, Keith is acting like a little brat.

You've Tried Threats. You've Tried bribes. But no matter what you say or do, Keith won't calm down.

I Do

The reason Keith is being such a pain is because of the truth of Psalm 51:5. Every one of us was born a sinner. From the Time we were Two months old and made our first choice To ignore our parents, we've been making Tons of bad decisions, decisions that fall short of God's plan for us.

Think right now of a decision you've made in the last 24 hours (or maybe even in the last Two hours!) That has fallen short of God's plan, and ask God To forgive you. He will. You can count on it.

FOLD HERE -

DAY 4

FAST FACTS

In one sentence, God says a Ton of Things That we need To know. Flip open To 1 John 1:10 To see what it is.

God Says

Your dad is home from work and walking Through your front door. You know you're going To be in major Trouble; you spilled grape juice on the living-room couch—and it's not just any old couch. Your family has only had it for Two months and your stepmom warned you not To drink anything in The living-room. Since neither of your parents were home, you figured you could just be careful, but you figured wrong.

Your dad sees The couch and asks you what happened. You start To make up all kinds of stories: Maybe he spilled it This morning and forgot; maybe it just Turned purple on its own. New couches can do That, you know! Maybe a bunch of grapes just spontaneously exploded.

He looks at you, and you know he's not buying any of it. "If you had just Told me the Truth," he explains, "I wouldn't be so angry."

I Do

When someone catches you doing something wrong, don't deny it. First John 1:10 lets us know that ALL of us are sinners. We ALL do dumb, wrong, careless and stupid Things. Today when you get caught doing something wrong, don't pretend you didn't do it. Don't make God a liar, not To mention yourself. Admit it. Confess it—To others and To God. And ask for forgiveness.

Pulse

FAST FACTS

If you want to learn how to get along with your friends better, dive into Matthew 18:15-17.

God Says

Let's say someone at school is spreading gossip about you, should you...

- Put an ad in the school newspaper to let everyone know it's not true?

- Go and talk to him directly yourself—alone?

- Take a poll in your second-period English class to see what everyone else thinks you should do?

- Sit with four friends at lunch and figure out the meanest nickname you can call him?

What is wrong with telling others first?

When does Jesus think it's OK to tell a few others about your problem?

I Do

Is there anyone who has done something mean or hurtful to you, either recently or way in the past?

When can you go to that person and talk with him or her about it?

FOLD HERE

QUICK QUESTIONS

Quick. Get out your Bible and read what God says to you in Hebrews 10:26.

God Says

What happens if we keep on sinning even if we know we shouldn't?

This is a pretty heavy verse. What is one word that describes how you feel about what it says? Why did you choose that word?

Now think about the truth that coming to know Jesus Christ as Savior and asking Him for forgiveness wipes away our sins. What is one word that describes how you feel after you think about that?

I Do

Can you think of a sin that you keep doing over and over again? Don't worry, everyone sins over and over again. The first step is to realize it.

How can you stay away from whatever is tempting you today?

SessionFiveSessionFiveSessionFiveSessionFive

The Big Idea

Grace is a gift from God that saves us from our sins.

Session Aims

In this session you will guide students to:

- Understand that grace is a gift from God, not a reward for their own efforts;
- Experience relief that they don't have to earn their salvation, but they receive it as a gift;
- Respond by specifying one way they can respond to God's grace in their own lives this week.

The Biggest Verse

"For it is by grace you have been saved, through faith—and this not from yourselves, it is the gift of God." Ephesians 2:8

Other Important Verses

Acts 9:1-22; Ephesians 2:4-9

Our Need: Grace

STEP 1 — MOVING IN

This step allows students to understand the difference between a gift and a reward.

Option 1  Move It

You'll need A big bag of cookies, a live worship team or a CD player and CDs and easily recognized music.

Ahead of time, set up this Name That Tune game by choosing 10 recognizable songs to use. **Suggestion:** Head to the local music store and purchase a CD with well-known TV themes (well known to your junior highers that is, not *The Dukes of Hazzard* or *Different Strokes* theme songs that you grew up with).

Greet students, then ask for three volunteers who really like music. Divide the room into thirds and assign each third of the room to cheer for one of the contestants. Explain that a portion of a song will be played. As soon as any contestant recognizes the song, he should raise his hand and give the name of the song when you call on him. If he is right, his team gets 100 points; if he is wrong, the next contestant gets a chance and so on.

At the end of the game, give out cookies to the winning team. Then explain that you've changed your mind and want to give out cookies to everyone. After you've distributed cookies, debrief the activity with the following questions: **For those of you who won the game, how did you feel when I gave out cookies to everyone else too? For those who didn't win the game, how did it feel?** Explain: **Most of what we get in life we have to earn, so when we are given something for free, it often feels strange. Today we're going to learn about something that is absolutely free although it's worth more than all the money in the world.**

Option 2  Chat Room

You'll need Copies of "Easy Earnings" (p. 76) and pens or pencils.

Greet students and distribute copies of "Easy Earnings" and pens or pencils to each student. Explain that students are supposed to pretend that they have earned 10,000 points by coming to church (or the meeting) today and that they can choose how they want to spend all 10,000 points that they have earned.

After they have finished making their choices, take a vote to see which things students chose most frequently. Discuss the following:

Is most stuff in life free, or do we have to earn it?

What are some things you have had to earn?

What has been free for you so far today?

Explain: **The things that were free for you had to be paid for by someone in some way. Parents, for instance, typically provide clothes, food and a place to live—these things are free to you, but someone does pay for them. In our culture, we are used to the idea of everyone having to earn everything. There's hardly anything that's ultimately free. Today we're going to study something that is completely free for us, although it did cost God something major.**

Option 3  Fun and Games

You'll need As many Ping-Pong balls as you can locate (ideally, at least one per student), some rowdy music, a bedsheet, a red felt-tip permanent ink pen, two chairs and candy prizes for everyone in the group.

Ahead of time, color 10 of the Ping-Pong balls with the red pen so that they are red instead of white. Allow enough time for the ink to dry completely before using them. Leave the rest of the Ping-Pong balls white. **Note:** Since permanent markers can have strong fumes, paint the balls in a well-ventilated room or outside.

Let students know you're glad to see them and then separate them into two teams, boys versus girls. Set up two chairs as if they were volleyball-net posts in the middle of the room—far enough apart to stretch the bedsheet between them. Ask for two volunteers to stand on the chairs and hold the sheet to serve as a net.

Explain to the teams that once you dump the Ping-Pong balls in the room, the goal is to keep their side of the net clear of Ping-Pong balls while hurling them over (not under) the net to the other side. Share that a few minutes into the game, you will be adding some red Ping-Pong balls that are worth 10 white Ping-Pong balls, so it's extra important to toss them over to the other side. Put on some rowdy music and let the game continue for a few minutes before you toss in the additional balls. There's no doubt about it, it's going to be bedlam; but it's also going to be memorable.

After a few minutes, have both teams gather their Ping-Pong balls. Do a quick survey of the number of balls and declare one side the winner. Distribute candy to that team. Then explain that you've changed your mind and want to give candy to everyone.

Ask the following questions: **For those of you who won the game, are you a little ticked that the losing team also gets candy? How do those who lost the game but got candy anyway feel?**

Explain: **Our culture teaches that nothing is free and that you have to earn everything. Today we're going to study something that is absolutely free for us. In fact, there's nothing we could do to earn it even if we tried.**

This step teaches students that our salvation is not something that we earn, but something that God gives us.

Option 1  Move It

You'll need Nada, zippo, nothing at all.

Explain how frustrating it can be when we can't do something. Ask students to cooperate with you to play the following "I Can't Do That" activity and follow your instructions. Begin the game: **If you can't whistle, move one seat to the left. If someone is already sitting there, sit on that person's lap. If you are at the end of the row, stay where you are.**

Continue with these additional "I Can't Do That" statements:

1. **If you can't touch your nose with your tongue, move three seats to the right.**
2. **If you can't curl your tongue, you have to move two seats back.**
3. **If you can't speak French, move six seats to the left.**

4. **If you can't stand anchovies, move two seats to the right.**
5. **If you can't touch your toes, move four seats forward.**
6. **If you can't burp on command, move two seats forward and three seats to the left.**
7. **If you can't drive a car yet legally, move three seats to the right.**

Ask students to return to their original seats and explain: **There's one thing that none of us could ever do, no matter how hard we tried.** Have them guess what it might be; then turn to Ephesians 2:4-9. Read the passage aloud and ask them to try to guess what none of them could ever do, even if their lives depended on it— which, by the way, they do! The answer is: They cannot save themselves!

Discuss:

What keeps us from being able to save ourselves?

Since we can't save ourselves, who saves us? Jesus Christ.

What motivates Him to do that? His love for us.

Can't we contribute anything at all? No!

What does God mean by "grace" that saves us? Grace is when God gives us something that we don't deserve.

How is Christ Jesus involved in saving us when we can't save ourselves? It's because of Him that we have the gift of grace.

Option 2  Chat Room

You'll need Copies of "Love, Paul" (p. 77) and pens or pencils.

Explain as you distribute "Love, Paul": **Paul often wrote letters to people he cared about. We have a copy of one of his letters to the Christians in Ephesus.** Ask students to take turns reading the letter aloud, one sentence at a time, while everyone underlines everything that God has done and circles everything that we do.

Discuss:

What are some examples of ways that we "fill our lungs with polluted unbelief"?

Is there anyone who doesn't sometimes do what they feel like doing, even if it is wrong?

If you had the chance to give a name to the "boat" that we all seem to be on, what would it be?

What's the difference between the kind of stuff that God does and what we do?

Why does God do what He does?

Surely we must have helped Him out, right? No, God had no help from us.

What would happen if we had a part in saving ourselves? We'd become proud and start bragging.

From what Paul has written, how would you define God's grace? Grace is when God gives us what we don't deserve.

What is the connection between grace and Jesus Christ? God offered His grace to us by sending His Son Jesus Christ to die and then be resurrected for our sins.

Option 3  Pulse Points

You'll need Your Bible.

The Big Idea

God's grace is absolutely amazing.

The Big Question

What's so amazing about His grace?

1. God's motivation is His love.

Read Ephesians 2:4. To try to depict God's amazing love, explain: **Let's measure love with sand. Our love for our favorite article of clothing is represented by a cup full of sand. Our love for our favorite television show is a bowl full of sand. Our love for our favorite friend is a truck full of sand. God's love for us is like all of the sand on all of the beaches and lakes around the world. Now** *that's* **a lot of sand!**

2. God makes us alive in Christ.

Read Ephesians 2:5-7. Explain: **Imagine that you were dead, then got to come back to life. What would you want to see first? What would you want to smell first? What would you want to taste first?** Share some of your own answers, being as descriptive and colorful as possible. Continue: **Coming back to life would make everything special which is exactly how we should feel about God's grace, since it also brings us back to life and makes our lives special.**

3. God's miracle is done without our help.

Read Ephesians 2:8,9, then share the following story:

Imagine for a minute that every person in the United States is taken to the edge of the Grand Canyon and told they are going to be killed unless they can broad jump the canyon. One by one, people begin to try, beginning with the least fit person and moving up to the most fit.

Some people would not have the strength to even jump a foot off the ground; they'd roll straight down the side of the canyon. Others who are in better shape might jump four feet. A high school athlete might jump six feet. The broad-jumping champion of the world might jump 25 feet. But no one is going to jump the canyon, no matter what kind of shape they're in.[1]

Explain: **The same is true for us when we're talking about saving ourselves. We can't! There is no way for us to reach the other side—forgiveness—no matter how much we try. We need God to rescue us. In Ephesians 2:8, we discover how God bridges the gap between our sin and His forgiveness: grace! God doesn't give us what we deserve. Instead, He offers us grace through His Son, Jesus Christ, who becomes a bridge over the canyon to cross from sin to salvation.**

STEP 3 MOVING ON

This step introduces students to the radical, amazing, I'll-never-be-the-same change from being dead in our sins to being alive in Christ.

Option 1 Chat Room

You'll need Several Bibles, copies of "Before and After" (p. 78), pens or pencils and a copy of a popular teen magazine.

Ahead of time, flip through the magazine and find a "Before and After" article, often focusing on weight loss, hairstyles or make-up makeovers.

Show the magazine article to students and explain: **We often like to see people before and after a change. Today we're going to look at someone before and after he found out what grace was.**

Distribute Bibles and ask students to read Acts 9:1-22. For variety, you may want to assign students reading parts, such as the narrator, Saul, Jesus, Ananias and the crowd (in verse 21). Hand out pencils and copies of "Before and After" and allow students to work in pairs to discover, then write down what Saul was like before grace, as well as what he was like after grace.

Ask students to share some of what they wrote in both the before-and-after categories. Discuss:

Why do you think God blinded Saul but none of the other men who were traveling with him? There are at least two reasons: He wanted to get Saul's attention because He knew the potential Saul had once he discovered grace. The others were eyewitnesses to the changes in Saul. Even though they could not see the light, it was obvious to them that something had happened to Saul.

Why did Ananias need to get involved? Couldn't God speak to Saul on His own? Sure, God could have, but it undoubtedly helped Saul to talk with an actual human.

Why was Ananias scared at first to go to Saul? He knew Saul's reputation.

Continue: **If you had to write a newspaper headline to summarize what happened to Saul, what would it be? Now rewrite the headline, making sure to include the word "grace."**

Option 2  Real Life

You'll need Several Bibles.

Read the following case study:

Oh no, you moan to yourself. You look to your right and who has Mrs. Greco, your English teacher, assigned to sit next to you but the school bully. You've never actually met him, but rumors have been flying about all of Greg's dastardly deeds. Of course, he's done the typical things like stuffing new students into trash cans; but he's done more, like entering the gym locker room, cutting off students' locks and stealing their wallets. And now he's sitting 24 inches away from you.

Why don't they just kick him out of school? you ask yourself. Probably the answer is because Greg is so smart. He's like the smartest kid in your grade and aces all of the tests.

Ask students this key question: **How would Greg be different if he found out about God's grace?** After they've shared their answers, explain: **The Bible talks about someone like Greg and what happened to him when he received God's grace.**

Distribute Bibles and ask students to read Acts 9:1-22. For variety, you may want to assign students reading parts, such as the narrator, Saul, Jesus, Ananias and the crowd (in verse 21).

Discuss:

How is Greg like Saul?

How is he different than Saul?

How might you be like Ananias to Greg?

How would the rest of your school react if Greg became a Christian and started telling others about God's grace?

Option 3  Tough Questions

You'll need Patience as you wrestle through these tough questions about God's grace.

Read Acts 9:1-18 and discuss the following:

1. **Why did God choose to show His grace to Saul?** Well, we can't know for sure, but one good guess is because Saul was so smart and a good communicator

that people would listen when he talked about God's grace. He was an educated Jew who was also a Roman citizen, which gave him influence among the Jews, Greeks and Romans, and allowed him to travel.

2. **What is the role of faith?** Faith is our response to grace. Once God overwhelms us with His grace, He inspires us with faith that leads to our salvation.

3. **What does Paul mean by "works" in Ephesians 2:9?** He means the way that religious Jews—like he used to be—tried to do good things to earn their way to heaven.

4. **What would have happened to Saul without Ananias? Would he have continued to be blind?** God would probably have caused the scales to fall from his eyes anyway, but you can be sure it helped Saul to hear from another human. Plus think of how much Ananias grew since he had to risk his life to help Saul.

5. **How come I haven't experienced God like Saul did?** God reaches every person differently. Maybe you haven't had stuff falling from your eyes, but God—the same God Saul experienced—is trying to show you more about Himself every day.

STEP 4 — MOVING OUT

This step gives students the chance to receive God's grace right now.

Option 1 — Light the Fire

You'll need A box that has been gift-wrapped, tape, copies of "God's Gift" (p. 78) and pens or pencils. Cut the tags apart.

Hold up the gift-wrapped box and explain: **This gift is like God's grace because it is good for us, it is something we don't earn and it is wonderful to receive. Right now we all have a chance to respond to God's grace. If you haven't asked Jesus to be your Savior yet, you can respond to God's grace by doing that now. If you have already asked Jesus to be your Savior, you can respond to God's grace by asking Him to give you strength in one area of your life, maybe even in your relationship with Him.** Emphasize that grace is not a one-time gift, limited to our salvation; it's a nonstop gift from Him.

Place the gift-wrapped box in the front of the room and give each student a "God's Gift" card and a pen or pencil. Allow time for them to write their names on the cards, then invite students who have decided to respond to God's grace to come forward and tape their cards to the gift.

Make it clear to students that if they asked Jesus to be their Savior, they should come and talk with you after this lesson ends. Close this time in prayer, thanking God for the gift of His amazing grace.

Option 2 — Fired Up

You'll need Copies of "Before and After" (p. 79) and pens or pencils.

Depending on what option you chose in Step 3, either remind students of the "Before and After" page or introduce the concept of how we have before and after stories in our lives that explain how we were *before* something big happened in our lives and how we are *after* it happened (hence the clever title "Before and After"). Distribute pens or pencils and the "Before and After" page and point to the huge "Grace" in the center of the sheet. Give students five minutes to briefly jot down how they were *before* they received the gift of God's grace by asking Jesus to be their Savior and how they are now *after* they received it.

Once they have finished, invite a few students to share their before-and-after stories. Then challenge the group to think about one specific area of their lives where they need to respond to God's grace by asking Him to send His grace to strengthen them. It might even be that students ask God to send His grace to strengthen them as they try to develop a better friendship with Him, for that is only possible by His grace. Finally, ask students to write a description of how they are now in this area of their lives on the "Before" side, then how God's grace would change them on the "After" side.

Close the session by inviting students to gather with prayer partners, both to thank God for the ways His grace has already been involved in their lives, as well as to tell how they want to see His grace more active.

Option 3 — Spread the Fire

You'll need Copies of "How Can I Get to Know Jesus?" (pp. 95-96).

Remind students of the important role that Ananias played, then explain that they, too, can be Ananias to someone who needs to know about God's grace. But being an Ananias takes preparation. We have to be able to explain about God's grace.

Distribute copies of "How Can I Get to Know Jesus?" Divide students into pairs and give them a few minutes to practice explaining the four steps to each other, as if one of them doesn't know Jesus yet. Ask each pair to close in prayer, praying for two friends that they hope to share the steps with during the next month.

Note:
1. Jim Burns and Greg McKinnon, *Fresh Ideas: Illustrations, Stories and Quotes to Hang Your Message On* (Ventura, CA: Gospel Light, 1997), pp. 55-56.

Easy Earnings

Take the 10,000 points you've earned by coming today and spend all of it by choosing from the following list. Make a check beside each choice, then add the points that you've chosen.

- Two new outfits   4,000 points   _____

- 30 extra minutes on the phone per day this month   1,000 points   _____

- A newer and faster modem   7,000 points   _____

- No chores for the next month   2,000 points   _____

- Getting into the college of your choice   3,000 points   _____

- A new car for the first month when you turn 16   9,000 points   _____

- Staying up 2 hours later each night for the next 3 weeks   6,000 points   _____

- Eating whatever you want for dessert this week   2,000 points   _____

- Straight A's this semester without doing homework   5,000 points   _____

- Being in the popular group at school   6,000 points   _____

- The haircut of your dreams through junior high   2,000 points   _____

- No fighting with your parents this month   3,000 points   _____

- A ride to school this whole school year   1,000 points   _____

- Unlimited TV for the next two weeks   2,000 points   _____

TOTAL 10,000

Love, Paul

Dear Friends,

It wasn't so long ago that you were mired in that old stagnant life of sin. You let the world, which doesn't know the first thing about living, tell you how to live. You filled your lungs with polluted unbelief and then exhaled disobedience. We all did it, all of us doing what we felt like doing, when we felt like doing it, all of us in the same boat. It's a wonder God didn't lose His Temper and do away with the whole lot of us.

Instead, immense in mercy and with an incredible love, He embraced us. He took our sin-dead lives and made us alive in Christ. He did all this on His own, with no help from us! Then He picked us up and set us down in highest heaven in company with Jesus, our Messiah.

Now God has us where He wants us, with all the Time in this world and the next to shower grace and kindness upon us in Christ Jesus. Saving us is all His idea, and all His work. All we have to do is trust Him enough to let Him do it. It's God's gift from start to finish! We don't play the major role. If we did, we'd probably go around bragging that we'd done the whole thing! No, we neither make nor save ourselves. God does both the making and saving.¹

Love,

Paul

Note:

1. Scripture quotation from *THE MESSAGE*. Copyright © by Eugene H. Peterson 1993, 1994, 1995. Used by permission of NavPress Publishing Group.

God's Gift

Before and After

After reading Acts 9:1-22, write down what Saul was like before he received grace and what was different about him after he received it.

BEFORE

AFTER

GOD'S

G

R

A

C

E

Devotions in Motion

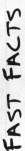

WEEK FIVE: OUR NEED: GRACE

DAY 1

FAST FACTS

Check out Isaiah 30:18 and get a glimpse of how God sees you.

God Says

Jerod's a new dad, just waiting for Scotty, his 14-month-old son to take his first few steps. Scotty stands up, wobbling but clutching onto the chair in the den for support. From the kitchen Jerod watches Scotty lift his left foot, move it forward two inches and put his toes down. Jerod is so excited. Then Scotty lifts his right foot, moves it forward two inches and puts his toes down. Only one problem: Scotty's toes are not strong enough to support his weight. Bam! Jerod sees him fall, and he runs to pick up Scotty, holding him to soothe his pain and his tears.

I Do

You're a lot like Scotty and Jerod's a lot like God. You're trying new things and you may or may not make it. But God's right near you, waiting to run in pick you up and hold and comfort you. Well, maybe not literally, but you can know this grace and compassion are all around you whenever you need them, including today.

What do you need God's encouragement about today? Talk to him about what's bugging you.

Pulse

FOLD HERE --

DAY 4

QUICK QUESTIONS

Dive into Hebrews 4:14-16, then check this out.

God Says

Jesus was a lot like you in lots of ways. What is one way Hebrews 4:14-16 says that He was different?

In three words, describe how God wants us to come to him

What does God give us in our time of need?

I Do

How do you normally approach God? Check all that apply.

- ☐ Whining. Thinking that will cause him to do exactly what I want.
- ☐ Shaking in fear. This is God, you know.
- ☐ Trying to manipulate him with all sorts of promises, such as "God, if you help me with this science test, I'll read my Bible every day for the next week."
- ☐ Walking up to him with confidence. After all, He's not going to do anything bad or mean to me. He just wants to hang out with me and help me.

How does God want you to approach Him?

What is one area of your life that you can approach him with confidence, knowing that He is a good and gracious God who wants to help?

QUICK QUESTIONS

Paul has some cool things to say to you today in Romans 5:12-17.

God Says

Romans 5:15 seems a little confusing. Who are the two men Paul writes about, and what did each of them do?

What does Romans 5:16 say that the "one man" brought?

How is this different from what Christ brought?

True or false: God gives us barely enough grace to get by.

I Do

Imagine God's grace is like a CD. He gives it to you and it never stops playing. What is one thing God would probably make sure was on the CD?

Pulse

FOLD HERE

FAST FACTS

If you have a problem you need help with, you'll love 2 Corinthians 12:7-10.

God Says

Your Aunt Mary Kay was doing way better, but now the doctor says that her cancer is back. Mary Kay is one of the most solid Christians you know, but you're still worried. You send her an E-mail to let her know you're praying for her and she E-mails you back. It's a typical Mary Kay E-mail. Very hopeful and quoting Scripture. She writes all about 2 Corinthians 12:9 and how her cancer has helped her rely on God even more. Her weekly chemotherapy treatments are constant reminders of how much she needs God and His grace.

I Do

Aunt Mary Kay is right. Think of the area in your life where you feel the weakest. It may be doing homework, getting along with your sister or brother or keeping up with everybody else during soccer practice. Ask God right now to help you to rely on His grace for strength. He will come through for you.

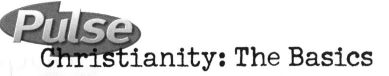

Christianity: The Basics

The Big Idea

We can tell God thank you for His grace by the way we serve others.

Session Aims

In this session you will help students to:

- Discover the difference between working as a result of receiving God's grace and working to earn God's grace;
- Experience gratefulness for all of God's gifts, especially the biggest gift of all, forgiveness;
- Respond by picking one way they can serve others this week as a thank-you to God.

The Biggest Verse

"For we are God's workmanship, created in Christ Jesus to do good works, which God prepared in advance for us to do."
Ephesians 2:10

Other Important Verses

Acts 20:17-38; Ephesians 2:1-9

Our Response: Gratitude

STEP
MOVING IN

This step helps students realize how much they have to be grateful for.

Option 1  Move It

You'll need Some candy prizes, one copy of "What Does It Start With?" (p. 91) for every two students and pens or pencils.

Greet students with enthusiasm and divide them into pairs. Explain that you are grateful for every single one of them and that you're wondering what they are grateful for today. Give each pair a copy of "What Does It Start With?" and a pen or pencil. Explain that you are going to yell out a letter of the alphabet. Each pair is to fill in the boxes by coming up with an animal, place or drink that starts with that letter (for proper names the letter may start either the person's first or last name). Good letter choices are *D*, *L*, *P*, *R* and *S*. The pair with the most answers that do not match anyone else's is the winner. Ask the winning pair to share their two favorite answers.

Since you have three columns, repeat this two more times with different letters and different winning pairs. Give all three winning pairs candy prizes.

Discuss the following:

Why is it sometimes hard to think of things we're grateful for?

Besides Thanksgiving, what are some others times when you are thankful?

Today we're going to learn how to show tons of thanks each and every day.

Option 2  Chat Room

You'll need A watch and a candy prize.

Greet students warmly, expressing how grateful you are that each one has come today and explain that you're wondering what junior highers are grateful for. Ask for a volunteer to come forward. Once that student comes forward, give that student a letter of the alphabet—we recommend *D*, *L*, *P*, *R* or *S*—and 45 seconds to come up with as many things that they're grateful for that start with that letter. For example, the letter *D* could prompt students to say they're thankful for dogs, dalmations, dresses, donuts, etc. You'll have to use your best judgment, because students are sure to stretch it (i.e., damp socks or dark computer screens)!

Keep track of how many words the first student listed, then ask for additional volunteers to repeat the process with different letters. You can make it even more interesting by asking members of your adult team to volunteer also. After three to five volunteers have competed, award the candy prize to the one who came up with the most words.

Ask the contestants: **Why was it hard to think of things you're grateful for?**

Ask everyone: **Other than Thanksgiving, do we ever try that hard to be grateful?**

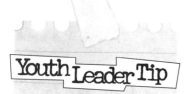

Youth Leader Tip

Whenever you can delegate anything to a student, don't hesitate to do it. Counting items on a list, keeping track of time on a stopwatch or writing responses on the board are all great ways that most any student can feel more involved and, in fact, be more involved in your ministry. It might sound strange, but handing a seventh grader a stopwatch is like handing him or her a part of the ministry.

Are you more or less grateful than you were three years ago? Why?

Think about your parents and all they do for you. When is the last time you showed your gratitude to them?

And what about God? He's done more for you than even your parents. When is the last time you thanked God for something?

Continue: **Today we're going to learn how to show our gratitude every day.**

Option 3  Fun and Games

You'll need A room that can be darkened, plastic tarps, trash bags, masking tape, *non-toxic* neon glow sticks (available at drug, hardware or discount stores), approximately three regular-sized marshmallows per student and rowdy music.

> CAUTION
>
> Use only glow sticks labeled *nontoxic* for this exercise and instruct students not to eat the marshmallows!

Ahead of time, place a line of masking tape down the center of the floor of the meeting room to divide it into two sections. Also, put tape around any poles that may be in the center of your room. Thirty minutes before the meeting, break open the neon glow sticks and rub their paint contents on the tape. Place all of the marshmallows in trash bags and pour the contents of the glow sticks inside the bags, making sure to keep any broken pieces of plastic from the glow stick containers out of the bags. Shake the marshmallows until they are coated in neon paint. Be sure to apply the glowing paint to the tape and marshmallows no more than 30 minutes before the meeting for the brightest glow!

Greet students with enthusiasm and explain that today they're going to start with a wild came called "Intergalactic Snowball Wars." Divide students into two teams. The goal of this snowball war is to get as much snow as possible onto the other team's side. Explain that this snowball war is going to be unlike any other they've ever had because the snowballs are radically different. Before you bring out the "snowballs," explain the rules: Each team must stay on its own side of the room; all players must stay on their knees and no snowballs—repeat— *no* snowballs can be eaten.

Lay down the plastic tarp (to prevent the church janitor from being greeted the next morning with the ever popular neon-marshmallows-crushed-into-carpet mess) and bring out the snowballs (a.k.a., the neon-colored marshmallows). Divide them into heaps that you place around the room.

Turn on rowdy music, turn off the lights and let the marshmallows fly! It's a good idea to leave a small light on so that students aren't colliding into each other in the pitch dark. After a few minutes, turn the lights back on and let both teams regroup. Then flip the lights off and let the snowball fight resume.

After a few more minutes, end the game by having students collect all the marshmallows, piling them up at the front of the tarp. Once you've collected all of the marshmallows, turn the lights back on and explain: **Today we used marshmallows a little differently than we normally do; we threw them at each other. Normally, we love marshmallows and think it's cool whenever someone gives us some. In fact, normally we thank people who give us marshmallows. Granted, they're normally not being hurled at us as projectiles.**

Ask: **What are some times that we thank people? What are some times we tend to forget to thank people for things they've done for us or have given us?** Answers might include a mom who makes dinner every night, a brother who gives a ride home from soccer practice or a friend who helps with Spanish homework. Explain: **The bummer is that more than just forgetting to thank the people we know, we often forget to thank God for all that He's done for us. Today we're going to learn how we can thank God every day.**

This step teaches students that we do not do works in order to be saved, but because we are saved, His grace makes us want to do good works.

Option 1  Move It

You'll need Several Bibles, a timer, paper, pens or pencils and candy prizes.

Explain that you're going to do a "Get To" or "Got To" activity and ask students to divide into pairs. Distribute paper and pens or pencils to each pair as you ask for a student volunteer. You will whisper into the volunteer's ear one of the tasks listed below and he has to act for five seconds either like he "gets to" do the activity—meaning he wants to do it—or he has "got to" do it—meaning he hates doing it.

Each pair then writes their guess about the activity he/she was acting out as well as whether he/she was acting out a "got to" do activity or a "get to" do activity. Continue to ask for additional volunteers to act out the following list of tasks as the pairs write their guesses:

Marching in the drill team for your school	Playing the piano
Reading your Bible and praying	Playing basketball in P. E.
Watching an action-packed movie	Cleaning your room
Taking a dog for a walk	Making a pizza

Award a candy prize to the pair that guessed the most answers correctly. Ask: **What is the key difference between feeling like we *get* to do something and feeling like we've *got* to do something?** The answer is motivation. Read Ephesians 2:1-10 and explain: **Paul's motivation to do all of the wild stuff he did was that he wanted to serve God because he had received God's grace. That's how it is with us today; we serve God because we're so psyched about His grace.**

Option 2  Chat Room

You'll need Several Bibles.

Explain that often when we have a crush on someone, we'll do some pretty zany things. Ask one student to read the following description:

My name is Ruth and I'm a college student. I dated a few people during my senior year in high school, but the college scene is *way* better for dating. There's tons of guys here, but there's one special guy that I can't get over. His name is Pat and he's a guitar player in a band and he is *so* cool. I'm trying to figure out how I can get his attention and let him know I even exist.

I was thinking I could write a love note and leave it under his dorm-room door. Or maybe I could "accidentally" trip him. Or I could put a sign on my car, "If you're Pat Figueroa, then I'm available." Or I could take my car and bump it into his in the parking lot, you know, "accidentally." Or I could maybe invite him to our next school banquet. Or maybe I could sprain my ankle, you know, "accidentally."

Thank the reader and ask students: **What do you think of Ruth's plan? What kind of advice would you give to her if she were your friend?**

Lots of times, we act like Ruth. Maybe we're not trying to do things to get the attention of a guy or girl, but we're trying to get the attention of our parents or our teachers. And sometimes we do things to try to get God to like us. What are some things we do that we sometimes think will cause God to like us more? Answers might include praying, reading the Bible and going to church. **Is there any-**

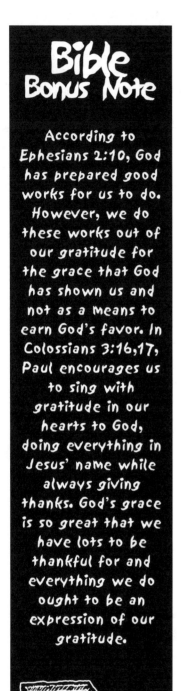

Bible Bonus Note

According to Ephesians 2:10, God has prepared good works for us to do. However, we do these works out of our gratitude for the grace that God has shown us and not as a means to earn God's favor. In Colossians 3:16,17, Paul encourages us to sing with gratitude in our hearts to God, doing everything in Jesus' name while always giving thanks. God's grace is so great that we have lots to be thankful for and everything we do ought to be an expression of our gratitude.

thing wrong with doing this stuff? No, because they're good things to do, but it's a shame that we sometimes do them for the wrong reasons.

Distribute Bibles and read Ephesians 2:1-10 aloud. **According to Paul, what should be our motivation for doing good things?** We do good works because we have recognized our sin, received God's grace and are motivated to serve Him.

Ask the same student who played Ruth to read the following situation, explaining that this is Ruth a year later:

> I can't believe how much I enjoy being with Pat. Not only is he my boyfriend, but he's my best friend. He tells me all the time how much he loves me and loves being with me. We do *everything* together, from studying at the library to hanging out at the campus coffeehouse. Whatever he needs me to do, I'm happy to do, like running to the guitar store to buy extra picks for him or helping him reply to E-mails that his band is getting.

Ask: **How is Ruth different in this second situation?** The answer is that she has a relationship with Pat and is motivated to serve him not to get his attention, but because she loves him and knows how much he loves her. Explain that the same thing is true with us and God. Before we know how much He loves us, we often think we have to do all the right things to get Him to love us. But once we know how much He loves us, it's easy to serve Him. In fact, we really enjoy serving Him!

 Option 3 Pulse Points

You'll need Something artistic from your house (a vase, a picture, candlesticks, etc.), two pens or pencils and two pieces of paper.

The Big Idea
Our relationship with Christ compels us to do good works.

The Big Question
Why does this relationship compel us to do good works?

1. We are totally unique.

Read the first part of Ephesians 2:10. Explain: **The word "workmanship" in the original Greek that this letter was written in suggests a "work of art."** Hold up something artistic from your house, explaining how it was made as well as why it is special to you now. Continue: **God feels the same about each of us; we are works of art that have the exact personality, body, mind and emotions that He wants us to have so that He can use us to do good works.**

2. We are totally called.

Read the second part of Ephesians 2:10. Explain: **We have been created to do good works. It's our purpose. We get into trouble when we get our purpose confused.** At this point, ask a few student volunteers to try to walk on their hands, which they may be able to do for a few minutes but not for long. Then give pens or pencils and paper to two student volunteers and ask them to write with their feet on the paper. Continue: **These activities don't work because our feet are created to walk and our hands are created to write. Likewise, we are created to do good works and when we forget that purpose for our lives, we get messed up.**

 STEP 3 MOVING ON

This step helps us realize that knowing God's grace motivates us to serve, speak and even suffer for Christ.

 Option 1 Chat Room

You'll need Several Bibles—enough for every student who might not bring his or her own.

Ask students to stand and line up in alphabetical order by their *first* names. Give a Bible to the first student, closest to *A* in the alphabet and ask her to turn to Acts 20:17. Once she has read the verse, ask her to hand the Bible to the next student, who should read verse 18. This continues until students have read through verse 38.

Distribute the rest of the Bibles because these questions require that each student has a Bible open and in front of him or her—although some of the guesses might be pretty interesting!

Discuss the following:

According to what we have read, what is Paul's primary task? The best answer is from verse 24: "testifying to the gospel of God's grace."

How did Paul try to live out verse 24?

True or False: Paul worked hard. Using Acts 20:17-38, build a strong case for your answer.

Paul had three main ways of testifying to God's grace: through serving, through speaking and through suffering. **Which of these three is the easiest for you? Why?**

Which of these three is the hardest for you?

Paul went through some pretty awful stuff. Why do you think he didn't just quit?

Imagine that one month from now, the elders of Ephesus want to send Paul a thank-you card. What would it say?

Option 2 — Real Life

You'll need Absolutely nothing.

Read the following situation and ask students to pretend that they are the person who is talking:

> Last month my mom was driving me home from school when all of a sudden this truck missed a stop sign and ran right into us. I remember my mom screamed, then she got knocked unconscious. I remained conscious and I could smell smoke coming from the back of our car. I knew I needed to get out, but my car door had gotten smashed and I couldn't move.
>
> This stranger came running up and got the door open with a hammer and then pulled out both my mom and me. About 30 seconds later, our car caught on fire. He saved my life and my mom's. No doubt about it.
>
> Now the man who saved my life has come by to visit us. It turns out that his company just went bankrupt and he asked if he could spend the night at our house and have some of my dad's clothes.
>
> Do you think we should let him stay with us?

Ask students to stand on the right side of the room if they think that he should stay and the left side of the room if they think he should leave. Have students discuss their choice, then ask: **Now imagine that this man lost his job and wanted to live with you for the next month and that he wanted you to give him $1000. Do you think you should do it?** Give them a chance to move to a different side of the room if their answers have changed. Continue: **What about if he wanted to live with you the rest of his life and asked you to pay for all of his food and clothes?**

Ask students who moved to a different side of the room: **Why did you change your mind?** Explain that when someone saves your life, you're so grateful that you're probably going to want to do anything possible for them, no matter what it costs.

Ask: **Who else has saved our lives?** Explain how Jesus has saved our lives. Instruct students to turn to Acts 20:17-38 and take turns reading the verses aloud. Explain that Paul was willing to serve, speak and suffer for Christ and ask: **Why was Paul willing to go through everything that he did?** The answer is because he was so grateful for all Christ had done for him and wanted to testify to God's grace (see v. 24). Ask: **What are some ways we can be like Paul and show our gratitude for Christ in the ways we serve Him?**

Option 3 — Tough Questions

You'll need A willingness to dive into these tough questions!

Discuss the following questions:

1. **What should we do when we don't *feel* grateful? Do we just stop serving God?** No, we keep serving Him, and ultimately He will restore our sense of gratitude.

2. **Should we still be grateful even when we're going through tough stuff?** Yes, God will never give you anything more than you can handle, and His grace will be sufficient for you.

3. **How can we be grateful in tough times?** We can concentrate on God's promise to walk with us through our tough times and look to Him for our comfort.

4. **Will we go to heaven even if we just receive God's grace and don't serve Him with gratitude?** Yes, although a true relationship with God will automatically result in a desire to serve Him.

5. **If we can still go to heaven without serving, why should we serve God?** Because we will be blessed and will grow in faith as we serve Him.

6. **If God is so powerful, why does He need us to serve Him?** Good question, but it has a wrong assumption. He does not *need* us to serve Him, but He wants us to because of all we learn when we do.

STEP 4 — MOVING OUT

This step helps students pick one thing they can do to show their gratitude for God's grace.

Option 1 — Light the Fire

You'll need One thank-you card for every 10 students, pens or pencils and tape.

Ask students if any of them know how to say "thanks" or "thank you" in another language, such as French, Spanish or Chinese. Explain: **So many times we're grateful to God, but we don't know how to tell Him in His language. But what we learned from Paul is that we can tell God thanks by the way we serve others.**

Brainstorm acts of service such as keeping their rooms clean, vacuuming their grandma's house or writing letters or E-mails to people who don't have many friends at school; then distribute the thank-you cards.

Instruct students to share the cards, each writing his name and one thing he can do this week to show gratitude to God by serving others in a tangible way. Collect the cards and tape them to the walls of the room as a visual reminder of the commitment to serve. Close in prayer, asking God to help us serve people whenever we can.

Option 2 — Fired Up

You'll need A copy of part two of the video *Schindler's List*, a TV, a VCR, paper and pens or pencils.

Ahead of time, cue the video approximately 47 minutes from the beginning to the scene where Oskar Schindler is overwhelmed by the opportunities he had to save Jews and didn't.

> **Note:** Portions of *Schindler's List* are not appropriate for junior highers to view. Although some of them may have seen it, don't cause yourself and your church unnecessary grief by showing the rest of the video!

Explain: **Often we have a chance to serve God and others, and we don't take advantage of it. Oskar Schindler was a German businessman during Adolf Hitler's reign who used his factories and connections to save over 1,000 Jewish lives during World War II.** Play the *Schindler's List* clip. Discuss: **How did Oskar Schindler feel when he realized all he could have done, but didn't? Looking back, what was he willing to give up to serve other people?** Explain how awful it is to realize we could have done more in a situation, but didn't.

Share that you don't want your junior highers to feel this way and that you want to give them opportunities to serve others even before the meeting ends. Divide students into groups of three, distribute a pen or pencil and paper to each group and send them out into the church's facility (or neighborhood if appropriate). Their goal is to cruise the church (or neighborhood) for 10 minutes, so they can make a list of specific ways they could be serving people that they see.

Once the groups return, ask them to share some of their ideas. Instruct them to close in prayer in their small groups, first sharing one thing they can do to show their gratitude to God by serving others this week and then asking God to help them with His grace.

Option 3 — Spread the Fire

You'll need A copy of part two of the video *Schindler's List*, a TV, a VCR, copies of "Serve It Up" (p. 92) and pens or pencils.

Ahead of time, cue the video approximately 47 minutes from the beginning to the scene where Oskar Schindler is overwhelmed by the opportunities he had to save Jews and didn't.

Explain: **Often we have a chance to serve God and others, and we don't take advantage of it. Oskar Schindler was a German businessman during Adolf Hitler's reign who used his factories and connections to save over 1,000 Jewish lives during World War II.** Play the *Schindler's List* clip. Follow up by explaining: **Schindler realized that there were people he could have served even more, but that by the time he realized it, it was too late.** Distribute copies of "Serve It Up" and pens or pencils to the students and instruct them to put a star by any places where they feel God wants them to show their gratitude by serving others (as they saw with Paul in Acts 20).

Close in prayer, asking God to help them serve the three specific people they listed.

NOTES

What Does It Start With?

Clues	Round 1	Round 2	Round 3
An adult I know			
A type of candy			
Something I eat for dinner			
An animal			
A place			
Someone in my grade at school			
Something that grows outside			
Something I can find in a shopping mall			
Something I can read			
Something I can drink			

Serve It Up

Put a star by all the places and times you think God wants you to show your gratitude to Him by serving others.

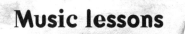 **Music lessons**

 ***During lunch***

My neighborhood

DURING SECOND PERIOD

During fourth period

AT home

Choir

Band, drill team or cheerleading practice

 My locker area

During seventh period

After-school sports

During third period

After-school clubs

During fifth period

During first period

AROUND MY TEACHERS

DURING SIXTH PERIOD

Of the places that you starred, list three specific people that you see in those places as well as one way you can serve each of them:

Name	One Way I Can Serve This Person
1.	
2.	
3.	

WEEK SIX: OUR RESPONSE: GRATITUDE

DAY 1

QUICK QUESTIONS

Grab the nearest Bible and spend seven minutes checking out Psalm 100. It may be short, but it's got a huge message for you today.

God Says

True or False: Most of the time God is good.

Can God ever do anything bad?

If God's love were a candy, would it be more like a Tic Tac mint or an Everlasting Gobstopper?

I Do

Write five things that you're grateful for that start with the first letter of your name. (Our apologies to all of the Quincys and Zeldas out there.)

What are the three biggest things in your life that you are thankful to God for?

Pulse

--- FOLD HERE ---

DAY 4

FAST FACTS

Flip open to 1 Thessalonians 5:16-18 and check it out.

God Says

This had to be one of the worst days of your life. First, your older sister wouldn't let you into the bathroom, so you didn't have enough time to comb your hair. Then you fell off your bike on the way to school right in front of the three most popular students in your entire grade. Not to mention the peanut-butter-and-jelly stain on your shirt from lunch. And now your teacher has sent you to detention because he caught you passing a note during homeroom.

It's OK with God to be miserable after this no good, very bad, awful, rotten, stinky, cruddy day, right? Actually, not really. He wants us to be grateful no matter what we're going through. At least you own a bike and at least you had food to eat at lunch—lots of people don't even have that much.

I Do

God's not kidding when he says be thankful in "all" circumstances. We are to give thanks in everything, not necessarily for everything (see 1 Thessalonians 5:16-18). Think of the worst thing happening in your life and find two things to be thankful about today. You may be grounded, but at least you can see your friends at school. You may have a cold, but at least you have some medicine to help you feel better. Think hard and you'll find there is always at least one thing to be grateful for.

FAST FACTS

Don't just sit there. Check out Ephesians 6:7,8.

God Says

When you do some extra studying for your history class, you're trying to please your teacher, right? Or when you vacuum the family room without complaining, you're trying to please your parents, right? Not exactly. There's a bigger audience. God is always watching you, ready to cheer you on whatever you do to help or please others, remember that your heavenly Father is the most important audience.

I Do.

Think of two things you can do today to serve people. When you're doing them, remind yourself, God is my biggest and ultimate audience.

FOLD HERE -

QUICK QUESTIONS

If you really understand Philippians 4:4-7, you'll have a much better day.

God Says

God's Word makes it clear that being thankful is pretty important. Why do you think being thankful is so important when you pray and talk with God?

How does being thankful make you less stressed out?

According to Philippians 4:4-7, being grateful leads to...

- ☐ a. Less anxiety.
- ☐ b. More peace.
- ☐ c. A huge turkey feast with mashed potatoes, gravy, stuffing, cranberries, pumpkin pie and whipped cream.
- ☐ d. a and b.

I Do.

Pick your favorite sentence in the passage and rewrite it in your own words.

Think about the toughest area of your life right now. How can you be grateful even in the middle of this struggle? Present this request to God and let His peace fill you to the top.

How Can I Get to Know Jesus?

GOD'S LOVE for us is so great that He wants us to get to know Him. We can always count on His love because God *is* love.

"And so we know and rely on the love God has for us. God is love" (1 John 4:16).

OUR SIN is what separates us from God. We sin anytime we fall short of God's plan for us, which means we sin every day. Our sin separates us from God not only in this life, but also when we die. Without God's plan to rescue us, none of us would have any hope of feeling His love and His relief from our pain right now or once we die.

"For all have sinned and fall short of the glory of God" (Romans 3:23).

GOD'S PLAN of salvation is the cross of Jesus Christ. God sent His Son, Jesus, to die in our place so that we could be rescued from our sins, experience true life right now on earth and live with Him in heaven once we die. Jesus is the only way to be saved from the sin that separates us from God. Jesus said,

"I am the way and the truth and the life. No one comes to the Father except through me" (John 14:6).

OUR CHOICE to accept God's plan is all we need to do to receive the gift of salvation that rescues us from our sins. God offers this salvation, but He

On the Move

never forces us to accept Him; it's our choice either to ask God's Son to take over our life or to reject Him.

"For God so loved the world that he gave his one and only son, that whoever believes in him shall not perish but have eternal life" (John 3:16).

Would you like to make the choice to ask Jesus to take over your life right now?

Jesus loves you so much that you can get to know Him by praying and asking Him to take over your life. You can use your own words or follow this prayer:

"Jesus, I believe You are the Son of God and that You died on the Cross for my sins. Forgive me of my sins and be the Lord of my life. Thank You for dying for me and making it possible for me to live with You in heaven forever. Amen."

How Can I Get to Know Jesus?

Big Word #1: Love

"And so we know and rely on the love God has for us. God is love. Whoever lives in love lives in God, and God in him." 1 John 4:16

Big Word #2: Sin

"For all have sinned and fall short of the glory of God." Romans 3:23

Big Word #3: Jesus

"Jesus answered, 'I am the way and the truth and the life. No one comes to the Father except through me.'" John 14:6

Big Word #4: Choose

"For God so loved the world that he gave his one and only Son, that whoever believes in him shall not perish but have eternal life." John 3:16

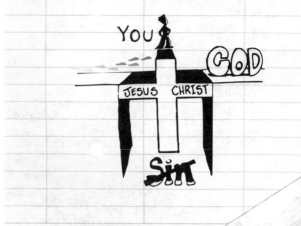

96